Rethinking Islamic Finance

Islamic finance's phenomenal growth owes to the Shariah compliant nature of its financial instruments. Shariah forbids the charging of interest (Riba) and instead promulgates risk-sharing and trade-based modes of financing. The Islamic financial industry has been subject to both critique and admiration. Critics argue that Islamic instruments (bearing debt-based structures) differ from their conventional counterparts only in legal lexicon and not in economic impact. The admirers argue that such instruments, irrespective of wider economic implications, rigorously comply with 'juristically sound' Islamic principles.

This book aims to reconcile the above dispute. It argues that the financial impact of instruments is a consequence of the way they are priced and structured. The similarity in pricing and structures is an outcome not of the underlying Islamic financial modes but of the competitive environment in which Islamic instruments compete. Even risk-sharing and trade-based Islamic structures, if implemented in such an environment, would have a financial impact similar to that of conventional instruments.

This book has a wider appeal for both academic and non-academic audiences. It can complement undergraduate and graduate courses as an additional reading on the intricacies of Islamic financial instruments and markets. For PhD students, it would help identify future research areas. To non-academics, it offers a deeper understanding regarding the working of the Islamic finance industry.

Ayesha Bhatti is an Assistant Professor at the Lahore University of Management Sciences (LUMS), Lahore, Pakistan. She is a Fellow of the Institute of Chartered Accountants of England and Wales and completed her master's degree in Applied Statistics from the University of Oxford, UK. Ayesha has been associated with the LUMS Centre for Islamic Finance since its inception in 2015 and has served as the Director of Training and Chair of the Centre. She teaches in the area of Financial and Managerial Accounting at LUMS and has written and taught several case studies in this area as well as on Islamic finance.

Saad Azmat is an Associate Professor of Finance at the Lahore University of Management Sciences (LUMS), Lahore, Pakistan. He completed his PhD in Accounting and Finance at Monash University, Australia and a master's degree in Economics from University of British Columbia, Canada. At LUMS he has served as the Associate Dean of Research, Director of PhD Program, and the Founding Chair of the Centre for Islamic Finance. He teaches courses in the area of Islamic Banking and Finance to undergraduate, master's and PhD students at LUMS.

Islamic Business and Finance Series

Series Editor: Ishaq Bhatti

There is an increasing need for western politicians, financiers, bankers, and indeed the western business community in general to have access to high quality and authoritative texts on Islamic financial and business practices. Drawing on expertise from across the Islamic world, this new series will provide carefully chosen and focused monographs and collections, each authored/edited by an expert in their respective field all over the world.

The series will be pitched at a level to appeal to middle and senior management in both the western and the Islamic business communities. For the manager with a western background the series will provide detailed and up-to-date briefings on important topics; for the academics, postgraduates, business communities, managers with a western and an Islamic background the series will provide a guide to best practice in business in Islamic communities around the world, including Muslim minorities in the west and majorities in the rest of the world.

Islamic Macroeconomics
A model for Efficient Government, Stability and Full Employment
Raja Almarzoqi, Walid Mansour and Noureddine Krichene

Dilemmas and Challenges in Islamic Finance
Looking at Equity and Microfinance
Edited by Yasushi Suzuki and Mohammad Dulal Miah

Islamic Social Finance
Entrepreneurship, Cooperation and the Sharing Economy
Edited by Valentino Cattelan

Rethinking Islamic Finance
Markets, Regulations and Islamic Law
Ayesha Bhatti and Saad Azmat

For more information about this series, please visit www.routledge.com/Islamic-Business-and-Finance-Series/book-series/ISLAMICFINANCE.

Rethinking Islamic Finance

Markets, Regulations and Islamic Law

Ayesha Bhatti and Saad Azmat

Routledge
Taylor & Francis Group
LONDON AND NEW YORK

First published 2019 by Routledge

2 Park Square, Milton Park, Abingdon, Oxfordshire OX14 4RN
52 Vanderbilt Avenue, New York, NY 10017

Routledge is an imprint of the Taylor & Francis Group, an informa business

First issued in paperback 2020

British Library Cataloguing-in-Publication Data
A catalogue record for this book is available from the British Library

Library of Congress Cataloging-in-Publication Data
Names: Bhatti, Ayesha, 1976- author. | Azmat, Saad, 1985- author.
Title: Rethinking Islamic Finance: Markets, Regulations and Islamic Law/ Ayesha Bhatti and Saad Azmat.
Description: Abingdon, Oxon; New York, NY: Routledge, 2016. | Includes bibliographical references and index.
Identifiers: LCCN 2018033003 | ISBN 9781472477675 (hardback) | ISBN 9781315606088 (ebook)
Subjects: LCSH: Finance–Islamic countries. | Finance (Islamic law) | Finance–Religious aspects–Islam.
Classification: LCC HG187.4 .B43 2016 | DDC 332.0917/67–dc23
LC record available at https://lccn.loc.gov/2018033003

ISBN: 978-1-4724-7767-5 (hbk)
ISBN: 978-0-367-66395-7 (pbk)

Typeset in Bembo
by Swales & Willis Ltd, Exeter, Devon, UK

Contents

Illustrations

Figures

Tables

Acknowledgements

This book is an outcome of many years of effort. It reflects the thoughts and ideas of the authors but in a way represents the collective consciousness of the scholars of our field. So it is only fair that we start with thanking these brilliant minds, of the past and the present, which have inspired and in many cases enabled these thoughts to be materialized. The list of these individuals would be long and for pragmatic reasons we refrain from mentioning any names. But our sincere thanks go to all those who have spent countless hours of their lives developing this field, in turn helping us to better understand Islamic finance.

We would like to acknowledge the generous support of the State Bank of Pakistan for establishing the Centre for Islamic Finance at LUMS. The idea of this book came about immediately after the inception of this Centre. The support provided by the research assistants at CIF-LUMS was instrumental in preparing certain chapters of the book. We would like to thank the editorial team of Routledge; they were extremely patient with us as we may have missed quite a few deadlines.

We would like to thank our families for giving us the space to finish what at one point seemed a herculean task. Without their support for our creative endeavors and the acceptance of the cost it may impose on their lives, probably we would have quit long ago.

Finally, and most importantly, we would like to thank God, for if there is one thing that we have come to accept in the field of finance it is that irrespective of our efforts to predict the future, it remains uncertain and beyond our control.

Preface

An important argument made in the book is that we do not live in a perfect world. Any utopian vision once faced with the challenges of reality is bound to lose the grandeur of the ideal. Those possessed with the keenness of perception can appreciate the beauty in the mundane, realizing that a utopian vision devoid of its glamour but implemented against the challenges of the self and the society may hold a value insurmounted by the perfect depiction of a false reality. We have held Islamic finance to this test in the book, where it tries to hang onto the sense of utopia while realizing the limitations of a competitive world. We also hold ourselves to a similar touchstone. This book has survived the competition of our attention. A book is mostly written with the blood and tears of the author, and this effort is no different.

Any creative endeavor is also a courageous effort for the authors to expose themselves to the criticism of the community, along with the realization that many of their ideas may not create an excitement in the audience as it had done so for the authors. There is something intrinsically fulfilling about the creative process though, when it creates the hope that the passion and the poetry may rub off on an avid reader. This book is a manifestation of our passion for Islamic finance; however, it may also depict our frustrations.

We have seen Islamic finance grow from an abstract idea to a market reality. This book in a way captures the story of Islamic finance over the last few decades as seen from the eyes of the authors. We hope that it will cause the reader to rethink the way they have come to understand Islamic finance.

Chapter 1

Introduction

What is it that differentiates Islamic finance from conventional finance? It is a question that has consumed many an hour of our lives. Some years ago, we realized that we might be asking the wrong question. A better question would be: Why is Riba (interest) prohibited in Islam? Only by rethinking this question can we rethink the Islamic finance industry.

When we started working on this book, Saad shared a personal incident that perfectly captured the real life implications of Islamic finance and of the academic research that is conducted on the industry. Narrated by him in the first person, here is the illuminating incident.

The paramount question is: Why is Riba (interest) prohibited in Islam? I found the inspiration to ask and answer this question in the most unlikely of places—in my parents' house, during a conversation with my mother's domestic helper, quite advanced in age. She had been working for my mother for as long as I could remember. My mother was very fond of her and would not relieve her of her duties, even though she was not as active and helpful as she once was due to her age. My mother felt as if she owed it to the domestic helper to help her financially, long after the transactional nature of their relationship had started to make little sense.

I remember that many years ago I was visiting my parents' house and the domestic helper was cooking for us. Out of politeness, I engaged her in a conversation beyond the simple exchange of pleasantries. I thought the conversation would not last long. I asked her about the village where her family lived and what life was like there. She spoke to me about the miseries of her fellow villagers, the abject poverty in which they lived, and the poor economic conditions. Making ends meet seemed to be the core purpose of their lives. Upon further inquiry, she mentioned their constant need to borrow money. I was now paying close attention. In my quest to support my theories with rich sources of quantitative data, I was realizing the importance of simple, everyday decisions relating to mundane matters by real people. I asked her why people normally borrowed. She replied that people usually borrowed money for either a wedding or a funeral. It was paradoxical that the need for the villagers to borrow heightens at the time of either immense happiness or grave sadness. Perhaps during these extreme states, the cognitive functions seem to allude us, and the rational mind is most subdued.

She continued suggesting that for most of their unexpected needs (or income shocks) they rely on charity, largely from their employers. When the charity is not enough or the want too big, that's when they have to borrow. She started mentioning an incident involving a relative who had to borrow money for his daughter's wedding. He borrowed around $1,000 (Rs 100,000) from a moneylender. The cultural norms of the celebration, the expensive dowry, and the grand celebration, all of these required a sum of $1,000. For a person who earned $100 a month, this was a hefty amount to borrow.

For the villager, getting the money was a matter of life and death. Without an awareness of the cultural norms of weddings in the sub-continent, it is difficult to empathize with the plight of the father. How far a distance from reason and rationality would the person be willing to traverse to ensure a happy wedding? The sociologist might call it an identity crisis, where the person sticking to the norms of the identity might be willing to bear a heavy loss. It seemed that the paternal identity was clearly salient. I wanted to test my theories, so I kept listening.

Who lent him the money? That was my next question. She started mentioning the dynamics of the money lender markets. There was a particular lender that she started to describe. She referred to him as 'a very nice person' who lends to people on a 'short notice' and without collateral. She described the borrower's happiness upon receiving the money. The picture she had created was clearly laudable, so I could not help but feel appreciation for the money lender.

My next question to her was about the rate of interest. The answer that I received changed my perception of the particular money lender and others of his kind forever. The rate was 50% a month. But what was more shocking was that she considered the rate to be fair. She said that the rate was lower than the market rate, making the transaction fair and the money lender merciful. I was caught between the exorbitant rate and the naïvety of the woman. My impression of the money lender also resonated between him being a hero or a villain, a savior or a destroyer, merciful or merciless.

Does the fact that the interest rate offered was slightly lower than the market rate make it any more just or ethical? If the borrower makes use of his entire money (of $100) to pay back the interest ($500), he would fail. He would either have to borrow more or let the interest be compounded on the excess. Clearly, he would be in a debt trap. Why did he borrow in the first place? How naïve could a person be? Or did the context of the wedding make it a good decision? What would I have done? It is easy for me to question the naïvety of the person, having never experienced the cultural context in which he operated. Not borrowing and not organizing a lavish wedding for the daughter might mean a lifetime of embarrassment for the family. Add to it the ingrained fear that in the absence of a reasonable dowry, the wedding might be called off or that his daughter might be subjected to humiliation at the hands of the groom's family. The social dynamics clearly favored the decision to borrow. But I was questioning the working of the market.

The market had correctly priced the borrower's needs existing in a particular cultural setting. In a way, the 50% markup was an efficient price. The borrower's desire for the money and his inability to pay (his credit risk) were well captured. A rate of 50% a month was the equilibrium price, where the market had now balanced the disutility of not borrowing with the disutility of having to pay an exorbitant interest in the future. The father's decision to borrow meant that he was well off; according to economic theory the total social welfare of society had increased. Beyond economics, the realms of ethics, fairness, and justice seemed to make the transaction welfare reducing. The ethical lens suggests that this man should have been helped. The society should have given him charity rather than convert his dire need into a business transaction. One does not need deep philosophical insights into the study of ethics to identify that it was a moment for the society to exercise compassion and the state to enforce regulations prohibiting the money lenders to charge the exorbitant rate of interest. At the end of that meeting, I was left with more questions. One question in particular was: What happens when the context changes?

Could the prohibition of interest only be understood in the contextual setting of a naïve borrower or is it universal? To answer that question, we set up a meeting with the CEO of a multinational company. The person was an extremely excitable character. He had the exuberance that had not subsided with age. With a strong sense of self belief, he had a glut of new ideas. Lack of capital seemed to be the only thing denying him his dreams—if only he could get the required capital. He was prepared to borrow from the bank at the market rate. He thought that his profits would quadruple in five years. The bank was only asking for 15% a year. The calculations made sense. Not borrowing meant giving up the opportunity to expand. At a personal level, it meant denying himself the possibility of achieving what he defined as success. This, he thought, would be unfair to him. He felt that no God would be that cruel to expect him not to achieve his potential.

The workings of his mind and morality were fascinating. He was right in saying that his projects had a high probability of success. This was no irrational exuberance. The analysts agreed with his predictions. Banks were competing for his attention. They were at his doorstep trying to offer the lowest rate. The CEO could pick and choose between them. Competition was clearly working in his favor.

Apparently, there seems to be little wrong with this scenario. It is difficult to understand why such a transaction could be unfair. The market is working well in this case. Any prohibition or regulation would reduce the societal welfare. The situation is in sharp contrast to the earlier case where the father of the bride was sure to default on his loan. Does this knowledge of a high probability of returning the money change our notion of fairness and prohibition?

One form of unfairness that has been identified in the Islamic finance literature is that of the lender. In this particular case, where the odds are in favor of the entrepreneur, the rate offered to the lender is apparently low. If the lender was a partner in a highly successful project, then the amount received would be significantly higher. Without going into the historical debate of what is more important for the success of the business—the lender's capital or the entrepreneur's skill—it seems unfair that the lender should receive such a meager return.

The two scenarios of the disadvantaged and the ambitious are at the heart of this book. As our sympathy changes with context, so does the application of the law and the emergence of Islamic finance products. The sociological and psychological aspects are of utmost importance to understand why Islamic finance products have emerged in the manner that they have. All the chapters in this book manifest the interplay of these different forces, including investor preferences, competition among banks, the risk aversion and biases of regulating bodies, and, most importantly, the functioning of the market. In this book, we hope to provoke a variety of ideas regarding Islamic finance. But we would particularly like the reader to leave with the message that understanding Islamic finance is not simply about understanding religious law or the intricacies of financial products. Whatever we see emerging in the industry is an outcome of sociological and psychological forces which affect the way the law is implemented. The sociology needs to be shaped and the psychology has to be understood.

Chapter 2

The paradox of risk sharing

Islamic finance is full of paradoxes. Imagination and practicality seem to be competing with each other. The imagination of the scholars, both religious and academic, knows no bounds. The writings of the early architects of Islamic finance abound with lofty ideals. The industry is presented as the 'alternative'—the answer to humanity's prayers and problems—capable of ridding the conventions of its ills. Islamic finance also has a champion: Musharakah. This financial arrangement, the birth of which can be traced back to the pre-Islamic era, emerged as the knight in shining armor, capable of slaying the evil beast of interest based debt with its strength and resolve. The ideals of imagination, however, were facing the rationality of profit. With the market as the judge, jury, and executioner, evil triumphed against goodness and debt against Musharakah. It seems that for the good to prevail and Musharakah to emerge, the hearts have to be pure and justice has to prevail. When the dark clouds of competition are replaced with compassion; when people are less fearing and more trusting; when the society and regulators collectively decide to penalize the exploiters with an altruistic punishment—only then could our hero triumph. Till then it would remain a privilege available to the courageous.

2.1 Introduction

The rapid growth of Islamic banking in recent decades has not been without its fair share of criticism. Many have argued that Islamic banks are actually not very different from conventional banks, and people have identified many similarities between the two. This chapter explores one of these apparent similarities by addressing the question: Why are Islamic banks more heavily engaged in financing models which are similar to those of conventional finance as opposed to offering the Islamic alternative of equity-based models?[1]

The underlying principle of Islamic banking and finance is interest-free banking. An Islamic economic system completely prohibits the charging of interest (Riba) as well as excessive uncertainty (Gharar) and gambling (Maisir). Each of these is considered to lead to injustice and inequality in terms of wealth distribution. Islamic economic principles, similar to a capitalist system, allow private property and encourage the earning of profit from trading activities; however, the fundamental difference between the two lies in the fact that Islamic ideology does not permit wealth accumulation at the expense of social injustice. In other words, ethics plays a critical role in Islamic economic decision making. Riba, defined as the predetermined excess payable in a loan contract, is strictly prohibited on these very grounds. On the one hand, the lender bears no risk of the investment and is guaranteed a return, even in the event that the project fails. This is unfair to the borrower. On the other hand, if the project delivers greater returns than originally anticipated, the benefit of this accrues entirely to the borrower. This is unfair on the lender.

In view of this, the preferable and superior mode of financing in an Islamic system is through profit and loss sharing models in which lenders and borrowers share the risk of investments. The result is a fairer and more equitable distribution of wealth which is at the heart of the Islamic economic system. Profit and loss sharing models, or Islamic joint venture (IJV) models, are commonly known as Musharakah or Mudarabah. These are the two types of equity-based financing arrangements offered by Islamic banks in which the bank provides funding for a project; however, there is no guaranteed fixed rate of return. Instead, the return is based on the profit—if any—generated by the project. Having said that, such modes of equity financing do not have a strong presence on the balance sheets of Islamic banks. On the contrary, experience suggests that Islamic banks are more heavily engaged in asset-based debt contracts, and equity financing is negligible.

2.2 Islamic instruments

The profit and loss sharing principle of Islamic finance is based on 'Shirkah', which means 'partnership'. Shirkah contracts are believed to be an ideal alternative to interest-based financing and are in the spirit of IJV. There are two different contracts based on Shirkah—Musharakah and Mudarabah.

2.2.1 Musharakah

Musharakah are Shirkah contracts in which the profits are shared according to a pre-determined ratio set by the partners which can be negotiated, whereas the loss is shared according to the proportion of capital by each partner. For example, Ali and Omer are two friends. They decide to launch their own business. Ali invests $200,000, whereas Omer invests $300,000. Ali and Omer are now partners and have contracted a Shirkah (partnership) contract. The profit sharing can be based on a pre-agreed ratio, but in the case of loss, Ali would bear 40% of the total loss and Omer would bear 60% of the loss in accordance with the amount they have contributed to the business.

2.2.2 *Mudarabah*

Mudarabah is a mode of equity financing in which one partner is a financier (Rab ul Maal), whereas the other partner, known as the 'Mudarib', pools in her expertise and skills in running the joint venture. The profit is shared among them in a pre-determined ratio; however, Rab ul Maal has to bear the entire loss. For example, a firm wants to enter into a Mudarabah contract with a bank. The firm has the labor and managerial skills to make the business successful whereas the bank agrees to contribute the capital. The firm in this case is the Mudarib, whereas the bank is the Rab ul Maal. The two parties agree to a certain ratio of profit to be shared among them, but it is understood that in the case of loss, the bank will be the sole bearer while the Mudarib will lose out on her effort.

2.3 The dominance of debt-based contracts

The risk-sharing structure of financing is not new to Islamic finance. Equity financing has been offered under the umbrella of conventional finance for many decades through venture capitalists (VCs). Venture capital financing, which has traditionally targeted potentially profitable start-up businesses in high growth industries, works precisely on the (Islamic) model of profit and loss sharing. In return for the high risk which they undertake, the VCs demand a high return. The VC structure usually involves some degree of control over the firm through active participation in the management of the project. Investment is made typically for less than ten years before the business can become publicly listed.

In the simplistic world of perfect information,[2] the firm (and the bank) would be indifferent between debt and equity financing. The payoffs under both options can be shown to be identical in a perfectly competitive banking sector. However, the perfect information scenario lies far from the reality in which lenders and borrowers operate in the world today. The dilemma in the choice between debt and equity financing options arises fundamentally due to this asymmetry in the information base of the lender and the borrower. Risk-sharing modes of financing demand a rigorous screening and selection process prior to accepting any project as well as their extensive monitoring. Significant time and effort (and hence cost) need to be invested in order to neutralize the problems of information asymmetry. When lenders give funds for a project, their knowledge of the venture is usually less than that of the firm (at least at the outset). The lender has to acquire that information through a detailed scrutiny of risks associated with the project. Only once an adequate level of satisfaction is achieved is the project accepted. Even post acceptance, continuous oversight is necessary to ensure that the project is progressing as expected. This comprehensive review process is required to overcome two key problems which arise as a result of the information imbalance between the borrower and the lender: adverse selection and moral hazard. Both of these make debt financing a relatively safer option for the lender.

Adverse selection relates to the risk that the lack of information by the lending party may result in an incorrect choice of firm, especially when it is costly for the less informed party to obtain that information. Adverse selection affects both banks and VC firms; however, their efforts to neutralize the impact of this issue differs. Banks generally try to neutralize problems of adverse selection through demanding high collateral or assessing the history of the firm, whereas VC firms adopt the rigorous process of screening and monitoring, as mentioned earlier, in order to overcome this risk.

Moral hazard refers to excessive risk-taking behavior by the borrowing firm due to the sharing of profit and loss in a joint venture contract. For example, those who have fire insurance may be more likely to be involved in a malicious activity in order to obtain the benefits of the insurance. Moral hazard problems can be overcome through close screening and contractual clauses enabling investors to withdraw their investments should the firm undertake excessive risk-taking behavior contrary to the initial strategy. Although banks are thorough in the screening process, they generally do not monitor the firms once the venture has started, which could lead to moral hazard problems and hence explain the focus on debt.

The risk from moral hazard can be neutralized to some extent. One solution is for the bank to develop long-term relationships with borrowers. This could take the form of spreading the funding over the period of the project (as opposed to releasing the entire amount at the start), thus giving the bank greater bargaining power by leaving open the option to cancel the contract and cease further funding if the firm deviates from the original strategy. Another possibility is legal punishment, which is a useful tool to mitigate the moral hazard problem of the firm misreporting its profits in order to yield a lower payoff to the bank. If the probability of 'getting away' with misreporting is high, the firm is likely to misreport; however, where there is a strong legal system which will impose a severe penalty on the entity if caught, it is likely that the probability of misreporting being detected will be high. Hence, the motivation to misreport will be low. IJV can therefore operate more successfully in such a regime, even in the presence of moral hazard.

Since the problems associated with information asymmetry can be dealt with, Islamic banks should be able to offer more IJV financing. However, there is another aspect to this dilemma which is not fully explained through the information asymmetry argument. This relates to the difference between the customer base of VCs and that of Islamic banks. VCs raise funds mainly through institutional investors whereas the customer base of Islamic banks consists of relatively more risk-averse depositors who in practice demand the sort of banking experience which is similar to conventional banks but without the Riba element. Therefore, in order to ensure that their deposits are 'safe', Islamic banks are more likely to invest in relatively low-risk, debt-based instruments. On the other hand, in return for investing in a bank with a high proportion of IJV financing, depositors would demand a high-risk premium, which is likely to be passed onto the IJV contracting firm. Since this will impact upon its profitability, debt financing would become a less costly and more desirable option for the firm. Ultimately, therefore, this will discourage the use of IJV financing.

2.4 Concluding remarks

The chapter provides an explanation for the dominance of debt-based contracts on the asset side. Possible reasons include the higher risks associated with information asymmetry between the lender and the borrower. Although these risks can be neutralized to a large degree, VCs are better structured to neutralize these risks through effective screening at the project selection stage as well as consistent monitoring through the execution stage. Furthermore, measures to neutralize these risks are costly in terms of time and money, and banks (including Islamic banks) are not necessarily best suited for the role. This gives rise to the preference for less risky (debt) modes of financing. Even if banks chose to employ various techniques to neutralize or minimize these risks, studies show that the predominantly risk-averse customer base of Islamic banks will result in the bank opting for a less risky position in terms of its investments, which may again ultimately result in the dominance of debt-based investments.

Notes

1 The inspiration for the chapter comes from a paper by Azmat, Skully, and Brown (2015).
2 For a detailed discussion on this topic, see Modigliani and Miller (1958).

Bibliography

Ayub, M. (2007). *Understanding Islamic Finance.* Chichester, UK: John Wiley & Sons.

Azmat, S., Skully, M., & Brown, K. (2015). Can Islamic banking ever become Islamic? *Pacific-Basin Finance Journal, 34*, 253–272.

Chong, B.S., & Liu, M.H. (2009). Islamic banking: Interest free or interest based? *Pacific Basin Finance Journal, 17*, 125–144.

Iqbal, M., Ahmed, A., & Khan, T. (1998). *Challenges Facing Islamic Banking.* Islamic Development Bank Paper No. 1.

Modigliani, F., & Miller, M. (1958). The cost of capital, corporation finance and the theory of investment. *The American Economic Review, 48*(3), 261–297.

Ueda, M. (2004). Banks versus venture capital: Project evaluation, screening, and expropriation. *Journal of Finance, 59*, 601–621.

Usmani, M.T. (2002). *An Introduction to Islamic Finance.* Hague, Netherlands: Kluwer Law International.

Chapter 3

Freedom from interest

Freedom is a liberty that our society cherishes—a badge of honor that we carry, demonstrating that the current civilization has triumphed. Any ideal presented in the guise of freedom is easy to sell in our age. It is not surprising, then, that 'freedom from interest' is the catchphrase of Islamic finance. The prohibition is portrayed as liberation—freedom from the enslavement of debt swirling due to the excess rate charged. The power of the compounding interest was challenged by Islamic finance. It promised an alternative rate that would be anchored in 'real' markets, and not the hyper-reality of finance. It would be fairer than the 'other' it aspired to replace. It brought the promise of blessings for the faithful and justice for all. If it were a human, it would have the sincerest of all intentions—a heart of gold. As the abstraction morphed into reality, when the Islamic rate emerged in the real world it took the form of the very evil it abhorred. A sheep in a wolf's clothing; maybe in a good way. The form is determined by the rules of the game and the norms of the market. It's like a beauty contest, where the inner beauty is of little value. The contenders are judged on external attributes. Creating a pressure to comply with the outer forms of the others, the inner beauty of the Islamic rate had to converge with the ugliness of the form it detested.

3.1 Introduction

Islamic banking is a term which is widely considered to be synonymous with 'interest-free' banking (or Riba-free banking). However, studies have frequently stated that conventional and Islamic banking are not substantially different from one another in structure and form. For example, critics argue that the benefits claimed by the Islamic economic system, of fairer distribution of wealth and of a more ethical economic functioning of society in which there is no exploitation, have simply not been met. One of the most frequently raised criticisms against Islamic banking is that the Islamic markup rate converges with the conventional interest rate. It has been suggested that the rates are so closely aligned that, other than the legal jargon and terminology, the two sets of products are as good as identical. These legal differences create an impression of differentiation which satisfies the Shariah conscious investor. Studies have been conducted which suggest that the Islamic rates are closely pegged with conventional interest rates, and hence the former are not *really* free from interest.[1] An analysis of industry data also suggests that the interest rate offered to depositors in the conventional setting is closely aligned with the profit rate offered to Mudarabah investors by Islamic banks and, similarly, the interest rate charged by conventional banks on loans is said to be in line with the markup charged on Murabahah sale.

This chapter explores this phenomenon of similarity of pricing offered under the conventional and Islamic systems. It also attempts to provide some rational explanation as to why this occurs, as well as looking at the possible steps which need to be taken to ensure that this situation does not arise and that the two sets of products are sufficiently differentiated in terms of structure as well as pricing.

3.2 Islamic instrument structures

As already discussed in Chapter 2, equity contracts in Islamic banks are primarily Islamic joint venture (IJV) contracts, namely Mudarabah and Musharakah. There are various debt contracts used in Islamic banking, the most common of which are Murabahah and Ijarah. A basic explanation of the structure and risk profiles of these key debt-based products follows.

3.2.1 Murabahah

Murabahah and Ijarah contracts are the trade- and lease-based contracts respectively, dominating the asset side of the balance sheets of Islamic banks. The basic structure of a Murabahah contract is based on the idea that rather than giving an outright loan to a customer, which is not permissible in Islamic law, the bank takes possession of the asset which the customer requires and then sells this to the customer on a cost-plus basis. The ownership of the asset results in the bank having risk relating to the asset, and this risk makes the transaction Shariah compliant. The ownership is for a certain time period, 'T', and in this time if the asset is damaged or destroyed, the entire loss would be borne by the bank. The bank is free to decide the payment terms of the asset.

Murabahah contracts may end up being more expensive than the conventional debt contracts due to the extra risk attached to them that banks have to bear. Furthermore, there is the additional compliance cost, such as the hiring of extra staff (e.g., Shariah scholar) or any other staff responsible for the transactions. As previously discussed, Mudarabah contracts are based on a profit and loss-sharing ratio, whereas Murabahah is based on a fixed mark-up. The mark-up over and above the purchase price incorporates an element of profit on sale as well as the risk of keeping possession of the product by the Islamic bank. Considering that the cost includes that of storage, transportation, and other processes involved before transferring the ownership to the client, the ultimate mark-up charged to the client could be similar to the conventional rate.

3.2.2 *Ijarah*

The term Ijarah in Islamic law means 'to give something on rent'. It can refer to the services of humans such as cleaner, lawyer, etc. It can also be used to refer to rent paid for the usufructs of assets and properties rather than services. This latter type is a similar financing arrangement to conventional leasing. If Company A wants to acquire an expensive asset, the conventional option of leasing through a financing house or bank will enable Company A to have title of the asset immediately but will require periodic (monthly) payments to the bank that has financed the purchase. The periodic payments comprise a proportion of the principal as well as interest. The bank does not bear any responsibility for loss or damage to the asset. In an Ijarah arrangement, the Islamic bank will have ownership of an asset and only its usufruct will be transferred to the other party in return for periodic rental payments.

3.2.3 *Mudarabah*

See discussion in Chapter 2 (Section 2.1) for an overview of the structure of Mudarabah.

3.3 Convergence of conventional and Islamic banking rates

If we do not consider the impact of competition, it can be argued that the optimal deposit and lending rates of Islamic banks are higher than they are for conventional banks. This is intuitive since Islamic banks carry greater risks as compared to their conventional counterparts—for example, the risk of asset ownership for the time period T and the risk of ensuring Shariah compliance. On the deposit side, the Islamic Mudarabah rate can also be higher than that offered to depositors by conventional banks, again due to the greater risk that the Islamic bank investor must bear. However, if we incorporate the impact of competition, the scenario changes. This is because Islamic banks function in a market dominated by conventional banks where the mindset of investors is already used to a particular type of banking experience and level of risk. In this type of market setting, the conventional bank is the price setter while the less powerful Islamic bank is a price taker. In a competitive environment, the Islamic bank will need to offer competitive rates to its profit-maximizing depositors and borrowers. These rates will be almost the same as, if not identical to, conventional rates.

The only way that the pricing of the Islamic instrument will be similar to the conventional one is if the risk profiles of the instruments are similar. To ensure a similar risk profile, Islamic banks will have to structure the product in a way which makes it similar to conventional products. If we consider the example of Murabahah, the Islamic bank, in order to remain competitive, can reduce the time period T so that the risk associated with asset ownership diminishes or even becomes negligible. Reducing T to 0 is not an option since this would make the instrument noncompliant. However, as T moves toward zero, the risk and structure of the product become closer to conventional debt and hence the pricing also converges with that of debt. Technically and legally, the instrument will, however, remain Shariah compliant. What can be seen here is that the competitive forces first set out to determine the price of the product, and, once the price is set, this impacts the structure of the product (rather than the other way around).

With the asset side rate converging with conventional lending rates, this will have a direct impact on the liability side. Again, the desire to remain competitive will drive the Mudarabah rate closer to the conventional deposit rate.

How, if at all, can this situation be resolved? Since it is the competitive environment in which Islamic banks operate that results in the convergence of both lending and borrowing rates with those of conventional banking, the importance of the role of regulators and Shariah scholars for ensuring that Islamic instruments remain Shariah compliant becomes critical. Islamic banks are clearly under pressure to price products in line with their conventional counterparts in order to attract customers. This is only possible if the risk associated with the instrument is similar to the risk of the conventional instrument. Since the key difference in the risk is to do with the ownership of the asset for the time period T, banks will be inclined to reduce T so that it is close to zero. Although banks cannot reduce T to absolute zero levels—since this would render the product Shariah noncompliant—even the reduction toward zero gives the perception of Shariah noncompliance, which is potentially harmful given the religious consciousness of the investors. Accordingly, the competitive banking environment requires regulator intervention to ensure that the structure of the products does not deviate from Shariah in actual or perceived terms. The regulator can set a time period T^* below which the bank cannot reduce T. If it does, it will be subject to a penalty. While the regulator does not know the value of T, it can conduct audits at random to verify that banks have not deviated from the regulatory threshold, and the penalty will act as a deterrent for the banks.

In addition, religiously conscious depositors also need to play a role in terms of influencing Islamic banks to have Shariah compliant products. They can do this by demanding an appropriate profit-sharing ratio on Mudarabah deposits on the liability side which will compel the banks to offer an appropriate mark-up on Murabahah instruments. Therefore, the banks' price charged to depositors also influences the setting up of a threshold price on Murabahah in a Shariah compliant manner.

3.4 Concluding remarks

The chapter looks at possible reasons for the convergence of the Islamic profit rates and the conventional interest rates for asset and liability side products. The main reason for this convergence is the competitive environment in which Islamic banks operate. Without competition, the Islamic Murabahah and Mudarabah rates would differ from their conventional counterparts due to differences in the risk profile. However, as soon as competition is introduced, the Islamic rates move toward the conventional rates. The phenomenon needs to be managed through regulator intervention as well as through Islamic depositors themselves demanding an appropriate return on the liability side, thus resulting in appropriate pricing on the asset side.

Note

1 For further details, please refer to one example of such a study in a working paper by Azmat, Bhatti, and Ghaffar (2015). The arguments presented in this chapter draw upon this paper.

Bibliography

Ayub, M. (2009). *Understanding Islamic Finance*. Chichester, UK: John Wiley & Sons.

Azmat, S., Bhatti, I., & Ghaffar, H. (2015). Can interest free Islamic banking ever be free from interest? (working paper).

Azmat, S., Skully, M., & Brown, K. (2014a). Credit risk in Islamic joint venture bond. *Journal of Economic Behavior & Organization, 103*, S129–S145.

Azmat, S., Skully, M., & Brown, K. (2014b). The Shariah compliance challenge in Islamic bond markets. *Pacific-Basin Finance Journal, 28*, 47–57.

Azmat, S., Skully, M., & Brown, K. (2015). Can Islamic banking ever become Islamic? *Pacific-Basin Finance Journal, 34*, 253–272.

Cappiello, L., Engle, R., & Sheppard, K. (2006). Asymmetric dynamics in the correlations of global equity and bond returns. *Journal of Financial Econometrics, 4*(4), 537–572.

Chong, B.S., & Liu, M. (2009). Islamic banking: Interest-free or interest-based? *Pacific-Basin Finance Journal, 17*, 125–144.

Engle, R. (2002). Dynamic conditional correlation: A simple class of multivariate generalized autoregressive conditional Heteroskedasticity models. *Journal of Business & Economic Statistics, 20*(3), 339–350.

Ernst & Young (EY). (2013). *World Islamic Banking Competitiveness Report 2012–2013*. London: EY.

Hasan, M., & Dridi, J. (2010). The effects of the global crisis on Islamic and conventional banks: A comparative study. IMF Working Paper/10/201.

Khan, F. (2010). How 'Islamic' is Islamic banking? *Journal of Economic Behavior and Organization*, *76*, 805–820.

Standard & Poor's (S&P). (2012). *Islamic Finance Outlook*. New York: Standard & Poor's Rating Service.

Usmani, M.T. (2002). *An Introduction to Islamic Finance*. Hague, Netherlands: Kluwer Law International.

Chapter 4

Financial crisis and Islamic finance

For many people, the recourse to God and the remembrance of God are occurrences during intense times of need. When the abyss of hopelessness reaches extreme depth, the light of God seems the only obvious path. Interestingly, the promise of Islamic finance—its ultimate fulfillment—is manifested during a time when the financial world is hit by a tumultuous event. The markets experiencing despair and misery. The plummeting prices turning the cries of the investors into the howling of fearful animals waiting to be slaughtered. Hope is avenged by regret. It is during these times that Islamic finance has appeared as a match lit in utter darkness, repairing the broken spirit of the rider who, experiencing the worst pains of the fall, is determined never to ride again. The fear of the fall has destroyed the resolve, like the fear of death might cause some to stop living. During such times of depravity, Islamic finance offers a reward that would stop the pain and heal the mind, the body, and the soul. Like all remedies, it is enshrouded in pain; the patient has to take the risk of not healing while bearing the immediate displeasure. The risk sharing contracts of Islamic finance offer a similar promise—at least in theory.

4.1 Introduction

Chapters 2 and 3 have discussed some of the apparent 'similarities' between the conventional and Islamic banking models. Given that risk-sharing contracts are considered to be the heart and soul of Islamic finance, Chapter 2 questioned why they are barely visible in Islamic banks and hence whether the two banking models are that different after all. In Chapter 3, another key point of controversy is raised as to why the pricing is almost identical for both banking models. Here again, instrument structures and their risk profiles come under scrutiny, and it can be seen that the true spirit of risk sharing was often compromised, making products somewhat similar to their conventional counterparts for the most part except in terms of legal jargon. Both chapters focused on the asset side of the balance sheet. Another school of thought, however, advocates that there is sufficient differentiation between the two models, not just in legal terms but also structurally. They take strength from the fact that in a number of different studies it has been shown, either theoretically or empirically, that the efficiency and performance of both banking models during periods of economic crisis is remarkably different.[1]

The roots of most financial crises have often been traced back to the conventional banking system. While identification of a plausible explanation is important, so too is the need to determine possible solutions. The intent has naturally focused on finding *alternatives* to the conventional model. Islamic banking, with its tremendous growth in recent decades, has therefore been scrutinized closely in terms of how it performs in troubled times. With reference to the 2008 subprime global financial crisis, various studies have argued that the heightened level of lending by conventional banks was the underlying cause of the crisis. This contributed toward the creation of asset price bubbles which eventually burst, resulting in an economic meltdown. The key reason for this is said to be the existence of *risk-shifting* contracts in conventional banking on the liability side which cause a surge of activity during periods of heightened macroeconomic risk, ultimately resulting in excess liquidity and contributing toward the creation of asset price bubbles. Since the primary instrument on the Islamic banks' liability side is *risk sharing* in nature, thus the liquidity inflow should be relatively lower during crisis periods resulting in a stronger and more robust banking system. This chapter discusses the two banking models by exploring the role that they play during periods of financial crisis.

4.2 Islamic banking, financial intermediation, and risk sharing

In contrast to conventional banks, where the financial intermediation role is largely debt based, Islamic banks are prohibited from fixed interest lending contracts and hence conduct their intermediation role through asset-based transactions. Islamic banks intermediate between borrowers and lenders through investments in assets, projects, and business ventures where returns are not predetermined; rather, they depend upon the outcome of the project. All investments are based upon risk sharing. The significance of risk sharing stems from the underlying belief that ethics needs to be an integral component of the economic system. An ethical economic system is one in which the distribution of wealth will be equitable and just. The system should have built-in mechanisms to ensure that economic fairness prevails. For example, *greed*, or the aggressive pursuit of wealth, without any regard to exploitation of the masses, is against the ethos of religion, and any mechanism which could lead to this is therefore also unreservedly discouraged. Inequity and a severe deficiency of distributive justice are apparent in most economic regimes around the world. Islamic scholars attribute the primary responsibility for this injustice to the dominance of the debt-based system and its key component of guaranteed interest. The charging of fixed (and often extortionate) rates of interest for the borrowing/lending of funds without any regard to equitable wealth distribution or exploitation is forbidden in Islam. These fixed interest-based products are *risk shifting* in nature. On the asset side, the bank shifts the entire risk onto the lender who is subject to the fixed rate regardless of how the project performs. On the liability side, the depositors shift the risk onto the bank because regardless of how the funds are invested, they are guaranteed a fixed rate of return. Conventional banking therefore provides depositors with a relatively safe and low-risk investment opportunity.

In Islam, considerations of justice and equity are paramount. There is no bar on owning private property, and there is also freedom to pursue profit. However, interest-based instruments, which are considered to be central to exploitation, are prohibited. Ethical considerations are critical in Islamic economics, and in fact the spirit of Islamic banking lies in *risk-sharing* instruments. While borrowing and lending are permissible, the truly Islamic method to conduct business would make sure that neither the principal nor the return is guaranteed. These will depend upon the outcome of the project. Islamic banking offers depositors instruments such as Mudarabah in which they receive a return based on the profit-sharing ratio agreed upon with the bank. Losses are shared in accordance with the ratio of deposits invested. In this case, the risk is shared between the bank (Mudarib) and the depositor (Rab ul Maal). The bank has the right to refuse the payment of the original deposit if the projects in which the bank invests incur losses. Pure Islamic modes of financing contain no element of Riba, Gharar, or Maisir. No party can benefit at the expense of the other. Islamic banks are therefore closer to the *real* economy, i.e., they are investors in goods and services rather than financial markets—this is in stark contrast to how conventional banking takes place. Since they make direct investments in the real economy, intuitively this should result in greater economic development.

4.3 Implications during financial crisis

This distinction of risk shifting versus risk sharing has significant implications for investor preferences during periods of financial crisis. Numerous studies on the causes of financial crises place conventional banks at the forefront of the turmoil. For example, with reference to the recession of 2000–2001, it has been argued that this resulted in several high profile corporate defaults which, in turn, increased the macroeconomic risk in the economy. Studies on the 2008 global crisis suggest that in the pre-crisis period (2001–2008), the macroeconomic risk in the economy had increased, resulting in risk-averse investors withdrawing their money from the real economy and investing in the banking sector, which was perceived to be relatively safer.[2] This perception may be attributable to the fact that bank deposits are guaranteed up to a certain threshold, or perhaps that banks are considered to have greater expertise in screening borrowers during times of crisis.[3] The redirection of funds into the banking system results in increased liquidity for conventional banks, which in turn leads to the agency problem between bank managers and shareholders. Since the compensation of bank managers is linked to the loan volume, they have an incentive to indulge in excessive lending by reducing the interest rate below the profit-maximizing optimal, thereby increasing the demand for loans and pushing up asset prices, resulting in the creation of asset price bubbles.

Islamic banks, on the other hand—with their risk-sharing ideology, the absence of deposit guarantees, and their relatively closer connection with the real economy—are expected to have more volatile returns at such times and hence are unlikely to witness the same influx of funds as their conventional counterparts.[4] Furthermore, the creation of asset price bubbles which occur primarily as a result of the agency problem and the discretion held by bank managers in reducing the lending rate, cannot occur in Islamic structures. For example, in an asset side Musharakah contract, the bank buys a real asset and then sells units of that asset periodically to the client at the market price. As a result, the optimal price is charged, independent of managerial discretion, thus preventing the formation of asset price bubbles. Consequently, the higher volatility of the return of Islamic banks' liability side during periods of increased macroeconomic risk actually impede the formation of asset price bubbles and hence economic collapse.

4.4 Concluding remarks

This chapter provides a different perspective on the discussion in previous chapters by highlighting the difference between Islamic and conventional banking models. It is the risk-sharing structure which results in Islamic banks having a more robust performance than conventional banks in times of economic crisis. This risk-sharing structure impedes the formation of asset price bubbles which are created by the agency problem in conventional banks. There is considerable scope for further research in this area; for example, the paradox of risk-shifting versus risk-sharing contracts. The former is generally considered to be of lower risk by investors, and yet it can increase the macroeconomic risk in the system. Similarly, risk-sharing contracts, which are perceived to be higher risk, may actually reduce the overall level of risk in the system.

Notes

1 For further details, please refer to one example of such a study in a paper by Azmat, Ghaffar, and Azad (2015). The arguments presented in this chapter are inspired by the said paper.

2 For a more detailed argument, see Gatev and Strahan (2006).

3 For a more detailed argument, see Kashyap, Rajan, and Stein (2002).
4 Azmat, Ghaffar, and Azad (2015), in their paper 'Islamic banking and asset price bubbles', support the assertion that in the pre-crisis period (2005–2008) when the risk was high, Islamic banks witnessed lower inflow of deposits as compared with their conventional counterparts. However, post crisis (2009–2012), this situation had reversed.

Bibliography

Acharya, V., & Naqvi, H. (2012). The seeds of a crisis: A theory of bank liquidity and risk taking over the business cycle. *Journal of Financial Economics*, *106*, 349–366.

Aizenman, J., Chinn, M.D., & Ito, H. (2010). The financial crisis, rethinking of the global financial architecture, and the trilemma. Asian Development Bank Working Paper No. 213.

Allen, F., & Gale, D. (2000). Bubbles and crises. *Economic Journal*, *110*, 236–255.

Askari, H. (2012). Islamic finance, risk sharing, and international financial stability. *Yale Journal of International Affairs*. Retrieved from http://yalejournal.org/article_post/islamic-finance-risk-sharing-and-international-financial-stability/.

Azmat, S., Ghaffar, H., & Azad, S. (2015). Islamic banking and asset price bubbles. Retrieved from SSRN https://ssrn.com/abstract=2618286.

Chapra, U. (2008). The global financial crisis: Can Islamic finance help minimize the severity and frequency of such a crisis in the future? Lecture delivered at the inaugural session of the Eighth Harvard University Forum on Islamic Finance held on 19–20 April 2008.

Cihak, M., & Hesse, H. (2010). Islamic banks and financial stability: An empirical analysis. *Journal of Financial Services Research*, *38*, 95–113.

Gatev, E., & Strahan, P. (2006). Banks' advantage in hedging liquidity risk: Theory and evidence from the commercial paper market. *Journal of Finance*, *61*, 867–892.

Hasan, M., & Dridi, J. (2010). The effects of the global crisis on Islamic and conventional banks: A comparative study. IMF Working Paper/10/201.

Kashyap, A.K., Rajan, R., & Stein, J.C. (2002). Banks as liquidity providers: An explanation for the coexistence of lending and deposit-taking. *Journal of Finance*, *57*(1), 33–73.

Chapter 5

The little difference between Sukuk and bonds

A world of grandeur has little appreciation for the little guy, someone who is not a celebrity and would not be recognized in a gathering of men. In a crowd he is indistinguishable from the ordinary, nothing to show and stand for. Spends his life in mundane matters. But the world revolves around these little guys. Standing together in their solidarity they display a splendid scene. This show of display could only be applauded by those with a keen sight and not by those with the untrained eye. If one gives a form to the 'difference' between Islamic and conventional finance, one would find an underappreciated little guy. A banal individual focusing on the world of the mundane. But as the real world, that has to be reminded to celebrate the triumph of the little, so too attention has to be brought to the significance of these small differences that distinguish Islamic finance. They provide it the much needed quality of religiosity. In 'Islamic finance', the word 'Islamic' precedes 'finance'. The grandeur of the ideology that promises salvation and justice stands on the shoulders of the many little differences.

5.1 Introduction

Sukuk are considered to be the Islamic equivalents of conventional bonds. The literal meaning of the term 'Sukuk' in Arabic is *financial certificates*. While Sukuk do have similarities to the conventional bond structure, particularly in terms of cash flow timings, there are some key structural differences which make them Shariah compliant. The fundamental difference lies in the fact that bonds are debt instruments which pay predetermined interest and in which the principal investment is guaranteed; both of these features are prohibited under Shariah law. Accordingly, Sukuk are structured in a Riba-free manner by providing holders with an ownership interest in some asset or group of assets. They are entitled to receive cash flows generated by those assets in proportion to their holdings.[1]

The global Sukuk market is currently estimated at $349.1 billion.[2] The first Sukuk, worth RM[3] 125 million, was issued by Shell MDS in Malaysia in 1990. Malaysia was also the issuer of the first sovereign Sukuk in 2001, following which many other sovereign and corporate issuances have been made in different countries. Sukuk have now become an attractive Islamic financial instrument for raising long-term finance in both Islamic and Western nations including Europe, South East Asia, North America, and the Middle East. The growth in the industry post 2001 was, however, marked by a period of slowdown from around 2008 to 2010. Two significant events took place at this time. The first was the 2008 global financial crisis. Studies conducted at the time and immediately following this period suggested that the Islamic financial markets remained relatively more stable and displayed less risk as compared to conventional markets. This was attributed to the structure of the Islamic financial products which, it was argued, made them less risky and more robust in the face of financial shock. A key feature highlighted here was the asset backing that they provided (see discussion in Chapter 4). The second critical event which impacted the Sukuk market at around the same time was an AAOIFI[4] pronouncement which came in early 2008 stating that most of the Sukuk in circulation were actually not Shariah compliant. The objections raised highlighted many of the risk-sharing features which should have been present in the Sukuk structures but were missing. This raised questions at the opposite extreme as to whether there was indeed any real difference between Sukuk and conventional bonds in terms of their structure and risk profile.

This chapter explores this question by studying the factors impacting the risk profile (and hence credit rating) of Islamic bonds. The determinants of conventional bond ratings such as firm size and operating performance ratios are initially considered and then the Islamic structural features are explored to see whether they result, as should be the case, in different risk profiles. In addition, process-related factors are also investigated, namely whether the approval of the bond by a Shariah committee versus an individual Shariah advisor impacts the bond ratings. Finally, industry-related factors are considered for their impact on credit ratings. Specifically, the impact of the AAOIFI pronouncement and the effect of the global financial crisis on ratings of Sukuk issued post these events.

5.2 Sukuk structures

Various types of Sukuk products exist in the market. This section briefly summarizes some of the basic Sukuk structures discussed in this chapter and the next. Ijarah Sukuk provide holders with the security of asset ownership, also referred to as SARA (Secured Against Real Asset) Sukuk. Musharakah Sukuk provide a risk-sharing model of Islamic bonds, also referred to as IJV (Islamic joint venture) Sukuk. Finally, Murabahah Sukuk (also referred to as Islamic debt bonds) are probably considered to be closest in terms of risk profile to mainstream bonds, providing neither the security of asset backing, nor the increased risk attributable to equity-like instruments. In Sukuk transactions, there are a number of different parties involved depending upon the type of Sukuk structure. Some key terms necessary to understand Sukuk transactions are Issuing Firm, Special Purpose Vehicle (SPV), and Investors (or Sukuk holders). All types of Sukuk structures will involve an SPV, which is an entity that acts as an intermediary between the Issuing Firm and the Investor. One of the tasks of the SPV is the issuance of Sukuk certificates to the Investors.

5.2.1 Ijarah Sukuk

The term Ijarah refers to a lease transaction. In an Ijarah arrangement, the lessor transfers the usufruct of the asset to the lessee for a specified period of time, but retains legal ownership. Accordingly, all liabilities relating to the ownership of the asset are borne by the lessor whereas liabilities relating to the use of the asset are the responsibility of the lessee. The rentals are determined at the outset of the lease.[5] The steps given below briefly summarize how these basic principles of Ijarah can be structured into a Sukuk:

i) The Issuing Firm sells an asset to an SPV for an agreed price (principal)—the asset is then leased back by the SPV to the Issuing Firm in return for periodic rental payments.
ii) The SPV issues Sukuk certificates to the Investors through which ownership of the underlying asset transfers to the Sukuk holders—the total proceeds received by the SPV is the principal amount and this amount is used to fund the purchase of the asset.
iii) The SPV makes periodic payments to the Investors which represent profit from the use of the asset—this is the same amount as that received from the Issuing Firm on account of rentals.
iv) The Issuing Firm promises to buy back the asset at a pre-agreed price. At the maturity date, the ownership of the asset is transferred back to the Issuing Firm in lieu of the principal amount. The funds are passed on to the Sukuk holders.

A simple diagrammatical structure of Ijarah Sukuk is given in Figure 5.1.

5.2.2 Musharakah Sukuk

The broad principles of Musharakah, as discussed earlier, are that all parties contribute toward the venture as partners. Profits are shared in a pre-agreed proportion between the partners while the losses are shared in accordance with each parties' contribution.[6] Accordingly, Musharakah Sukuk are structured by keeping these broad principles in mind. Both the Issuing Firm and

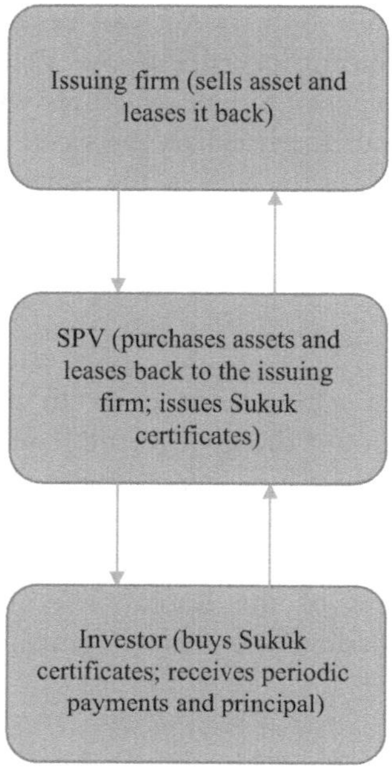

Figure 5.1 Ijarah Sukuk: structure overview

the SPV (on behalf of the Sukuk holders) contribute toward the project in terms of cash/resources. The main steps are given below:

i) The SPV issues Sukuk certificates to Investors and receives the principal sum as proceeds from the issue. The certificates entitle the Investors to receive periodic payments from the Sukuk certificates.
ii) The SPV (Trustee) becomes the trustee of the funds received in (i) and enters into a Musharakah arrangement with the Issuing Firm. The Trustee contributes the principal amount received from the Investors and hence becomes a party to the Musharakah arrangement in proportion to the contribution made. The profits are shared based upon a mutually agreed proportion while the losses are shared in the same ratio as the contribution made.
iii) On each periodic distribution date, the SPV receives a share of the profits generated by the Musharakah asset (or shares in the losses of the asset in proportion to the contribution made). This is paid to the Sukuk holders.
iv) At the agreed date, the share of ownership of the Sukuk holders is bought back by the Issuing Firm at the market price and not at a predetermined rate. In Musharakah Sukuk, the principal is not guaranteed.

A simple diagrammatical structure of Musharakah Sukuk is given in Figure 5.2.

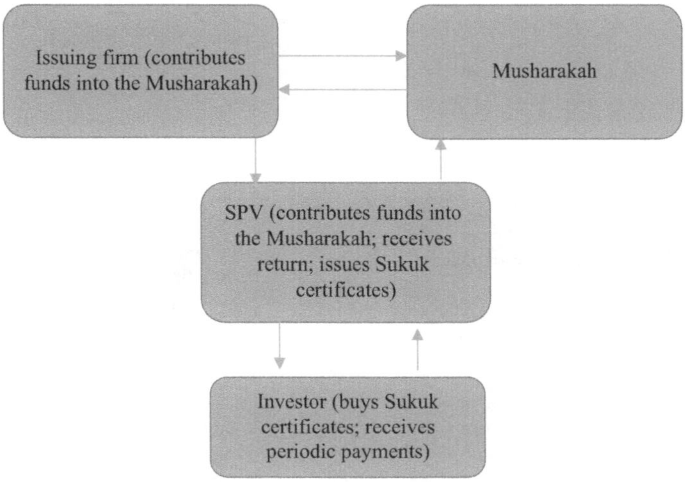

Figure 5.2 Musharakah Sukuk: structure overview

5.2.3 Murabahah Sukuk

Murabahah is a term used to describe an instrument whereby the two parties engage in a sale and purchase agreement of some underlying asset. The purchase price is determined and agreed upon at the outset and usually includes some form of markup on the original price of the asset, and the payment terms are often deferred. In accordance with these broad principles, the basic steps in a Murabahah Sukuk are given below:

i) The SPV issues Sukuk certificates to the Investors for a consideration which totals the principal amount. The certificates entitle the Investors to receive periodic amounts from the SPV as a return on the certificates.
ii) The SPV uses the funds received from the Investors to make a spot purchase of the underlying asset (commodities) from a third-party supplier.
iii) The SPV enters into a sale and purchase agreement with the Issuing Firm for the underlying asset, which results in the transfer of ownership to the Issuing Firm (on deferred payment terms).
iv) The Issuing Firm makes the deferred payments to the SPV periodically, and these amounts are paid to the Investors by way of return on their Sukuk certificates.

A simple diagrammatical structure of Murabahah Sukuk is given in Figure 5.3.

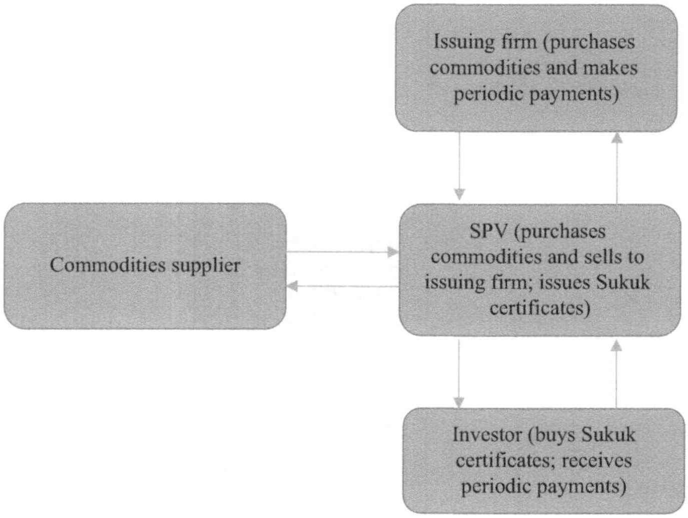

Figure 5.3 Murabahah Sukuk: structure overview

5.3 Determinants of credit ratings of Islamic bonds

Various factors impact the riskiness of an instrument. For example, the creditworthiness of the issuing firm plays a key role. Different financial ratios can be analyzed to understand their effect on the credit rating of the instrument. Further, the particular structure employed for raising funds (i.e., does the bond represent asset ownership or is it risk sharing in nature?) is an important component of risk as well as the external macroeconomic environment. To establish which factors impact the ratings of Islamic bonds, the following broad categories of determinants are considered:[7]

i) conventional determinants—various ratios (also used in determining ratings for conventional bonds) can be applied to establish their impact on the ratings of the different Islamic bonds.
ii) structural factors—the different bond structures, namely Ijarah bonds (with their underlying asset ownership structure) and Musharakah bonds (with their risk-sharing structure) can be compared to Murabahah (debt-based) bonds to determine if any differences exist in ratings owing to the structure of the bonds.
iii) process-related factors—these mainly test the impact of Shariah committees on bond ratings versus individual Shariah advisors.
iv) industry-related factors—two main aspects are explored. Firstly, whether the 2008 AAOIFI rulings resulted in more Shariah compliant bonds and

hence more highly rated bonds; and secondly, whether the 2008 subprime crisis impacted the ratings of Islamic bonds.

As with conventional bonds, high interest cover and firm size (due to the more established and diverse product lines and hence lower risk) can be expected to have a positive impact on the credit rating of Islamic bonds. In terms of leverage, long-term debt to total assets has a positive impact on credit ratings, whereas total debt to assets (including short-term debt) negatively impacts ratings due to the relatively shorter maturities of Islamic bonds as compared to their conventional counterparts.

In terms of the Islamic structural differences, the data suggest that Ijarah bonds, which should be rated higher than Murabahah bonds due to the fact that they represent asset ownership, are sometimes rated marginally lower. Furthermore, Musharakah bonds, which are risk sharing in nature and hence should be rated lower than debt bonds, are in fact rated higher.

Process and industry factors are also significant determinants of credit ratings. Shariah committee approved bonds are normally rated higher than those endorsed by individual advisors. Similarly, the 2008 AAOIFI pronouncements impacted bond ratings positively, and Islamic bond issues after the 2008 financial crisis were actually rated higher than previous issues.

5.4 Concluding remarks

This chapter sheds light on the determinants of Islamic bond ratings and compares Ijarah, Musharakah, and Murabahah Sukuk in an effort to answer the question: Are Islamic instruments *really* different from their conventional counterparts? Broadly speaking, the factors considered are various ratios (known to have an impact on conventional bond ratings), structural factors, process factors, and industry-related factors. Some of the outcomes are as per expectations; for example, in terms of the ratios, many of those having a positive impact on ratings of conventional bonds have a similar impact on Islamic Sukuk too (like interest cover, firm size, and long-term debt to asset ratio). However, some of the results are surprising and somewhat counter intuitive, particularly the fact that Ijarah bonds, which represent asset ownership, are rated lower than Murabahah bonds. In addition, Murabahah bonds are rated lower than the risk-sharing Musharakah bonds. This suggests that the substance of the structures may not be in line with their legal form.

Overall it can be concluded that in terms of their risk profiles, Sukuk have certain similarities with conventional bonds. At the same time there exist important differences from their conventional counterparts—in particular, the impact of process and industry-related factors that may affect the credit risk of Islamic instruments contribute to the uniqueness of this industry.

Notes

1 The inspiration for the chapter comes from the paper by Azmat, Skully, and Brown (2017).
2 www.mifc.com/index.php?rp=Sukuk_report_270317.pdf, retrieved May 20, 2017.
3 RM: Malaysian Ringgits.
4 AAOIFI is an abbreviation for *Accounting and Auditing Organization for Islamic Financial Institutions*. AAOIFI is an international not-for-profit body that prepares accounting, auditing, governance, ethics, and Shariah standards for Islamic financial institutions and the industry.
5 Usmani (2002), 160.
6 Usmani (2002), 38.
7 Azmat et al. (2015) investigated the credit rating determinants of Islamic bonds and tested various hypotheses. The data set comprised 458 corporate Islamic bonds issued in Malaysia between 2002 and 2010. Of these, 393 were Murabahah (Islamic debt) bonds, 17 were Ijarah (SARA) bonds, and 48 were Musharakah (IJV) bonds. This following discussion is based on the results of that study.

Bibliography

AAOIFI. (2008). Sukuk resolution. Retrieved June 13, 2009, from www.aaoifi.com/aaoifi_sb_sukuk_Feb2008_Eng.pdf.

Abedifar, P., Molyneux, P., & Tarazi, A. (2013). Risk in Islamic banking. *Review of Finance*, *17*, 2035–2096.

Ali, S.S. (ed.) (2008). Islamic capital markets: Current state and developmental challenges. In: *Islamic Capital Markets, Products, Regulation and Development*. Jeddah: Islamic Research & Training Institute, 1–22.

Altman, E.I. (1968). Financial ratios, discriminant analysis and prediction of corporate bankruptcy. *Journal of Finance*, *23*(4), 589–609.

Archer, S., & Karim, R.A. (2007). *Islamic Finance: The Regulatory Challenge*. Singapore: John Wiley & Sons. doi: 10.1002/9781118390443.

Arundina, T., Omar, M.A., & Kartiwi, M. (2015). The predictive accuracy of Sukuk ratings: Multinomial logistic and neural network inferences. *Pacific Basin Finance Journal*, *34*, 273–292.

Askari, H. (2012). Islamic finance, risk sharing, and international financial stability. *Yale Journal of International Affairs*. Retrieved September 8, 2018 from http://yalejournal.org/article_post/islamic-finance-risk-sharing-and-international-financial-stability/.

Askari, H., & Rehman, S.S. (2010). How Islamic are Islamic countries? *Global Economy Journal*, *10*, 1–37.

Ayub, M. (2007). *Understanding Islamic Finance*. Chichester, UK: John Wiley & Sons.

Azmat, S., Skully, M., & Brown, K. (2014a). Credit risk in Islamic joint venture bonds. *Journal of Economic Behavior & Organization*, *103*, S129–S145.

Azmat, S., Skully, M., & Brown, K. (2014b). Issuer's choice of Islamic bond type. *Pacific-Basin Finance Journal*, *28*, 122–135.

Azmat, S., Skully, M., & Brown, K. (2015). Can Islamic banking ever become Islamic? *Pacific-Basin Finance Journal*, *34*, 253–272.

Azmat, S., Skully, M., & Brown, K. (2017). The (Little) difference that makes all the difference between Islamic and conventional bonds. *Pacific-Basin Finance Journal*, *42*, 46–59.

Beck, T., Demirguc-Kunt, A., & Merrouche, O. (2013). Islamic vs. conventional banking: Business model, efficiency and stability. *Journal of Banking & Finance, 37*, 433–447.

Blume, M.E., Lim, F., & MacKinlay, C.A. (1998). The declining credit quality of U.S. corporate debt: Myth or reality? *Journal of Finance, 53*, 1389–1413.

Chapra, U.M. (2008). The global financial crisis: Can Islamic finance help minimize the severity and frequency of such a crisis in the future? Presented at the Forum on the Global Financial Crisis, Islamic Development Bank, 25 October.

Chong, B.S., & Liu, M.H. (2009). Islamic banking: Interest free or interest based? *Pacific-Basin Finance Journal, 17*, 125–144.

Dooley, M., & Hutchison, M. (2009). Transmission of the U.S. subprime crisis to emerging markets: Evidence on the decoupling-recoupling hypothesis. *Journal of International Money and Finance, 28*, 1331–1349.

Dusuki, A.W., & Mokhtar, S. (2010). *Critical Appraisal of Shariah Issues on Ownership in Asset Based Sukuk as Implemented in the Islamic Debt Market.* Research Paper No 8. Kuala Lumpur, Malaysia: International Shariah Research Academy on Islamic Finance.

EYEY. (2014). Global takaful insights: Market updates. Retrieved September 12, 2018 from www.ey.com/my/en/industries/financial-services/insurance/ey-global-takaful-insights-2014

Godlewski, C.J., Turk-Ariss, R., & Weill, L. (2013). Sukuk vs. conventional bonds: A stock market perspective. *Journal of Comparative Economics, 41*, 745–761.

Godlewski, C.J., Turk-Ariss, R., & Weill, L. (2014). Do the type of Sukuk and choice of Shari'a scholar matter? Banking of Finland, BOFIT Discussion Paper No. 21, December.

Grais, W., & Pellegrini, M. (2006). *Corporate Governance in Institutions Offering Islamic Financial Services: Issues and Options.* Policy Research Working Paper 4052, Washington, DC: World Bank, Financial and Private Sector Development Network.

Gray, S., Mirkovic, A., & Ragunathan, V. (2006). The determinants of credit ratings: Australian evidence. *Australian Journal of Management, 31*, 333–354.

Greene, W.H. (2003). *Econometric Analysis.* 5th ed. Upper Saddle River, NJ: Prentice Hall.

Hasan, M., & Dridi, J. (2010). The effects of the global crisis on Islamic and conventional banks: A comparative study. IMF Working Paper No., WP/10/201, September.

Hovakimian, A., Opler, T., & Titman, S. (2001). The debt-equity choice. *Journal of Finance and Quantitative Analysis, 36*, 1–24.

Howladar, K. (2006). *Shari'ah and Sukuk: A Moody's Primer.* International Structured Finance Special Comment. New York: Moody's Investors Service.

Huber, P.J. (1964). Robust estimation of a location parameter. *The Annals of Mathematical Statistics, 35*, 73–101.

(IMF) International Monetary Fund. (2015). *Islamic Fact Sheet.* Retrieved August 3, 2015, from www.imf.org/external/themes/islamicfinance/#Factsheet.

Iqbal, M., Ahmed, A., & Khan, T. (1998). *Challenges Facing, Islamic Banking.* (Occasional Paper No. 1). Jeddah, Saudi Arabia: Islamic Research and Training Institute, Islamic Development Bank.

Iqbal, Z. (1997). Islamic financial systems. *Finance and Development, 34*, 42–45.

Iskandar-Datta, M.E., & Emery, D.R. (1994). An empirical investigation of the role of indenture provisions in determining bond ratings. *Journal of Banking & Finance, 18*, 93–111.

Islamic Financial Services Industry (ISFI). (2015). *Islamic Financial Services Industry Stability Report 2015*. 3rd ed., May. Kuala Lumpur, Malaysia.

Kaplan, R., & Urwitz, G. (1979). Statistical models on bond ratings: A methodological inquiry. *Journal of Business, 52*, 231–261.

Karim, R.A.A. (1990). The independence of religious and external auditors: The case of Islamic banks. *Accounting, Auditing and Accountability, 3*, 34–44.

Khan, F. (2010). How 'Islamic' is Islamic banking? *Journal of Economic Behavior & Organization, 76*, 805–820.

Klein, P.O., Weill, L., & Godlewski, C.J. (2015). How Sukuk shapes firm performance. University of Strasbourg Working Paper No. 2015-05,May.

Marsh, P. (1982). The choice between equity and debt: An empirical-study. *Journal of Finance, 37*, 121–144.

Miller, N.D., Challoner, J., & Atta, A. (2007). UK welcomes the Sukuk. *International Financial Law Review, 26*, 24–25.

Mohamed, H.H., Masih, M., & Bacha, O.I. (2015). Why do issuers issue Sukuk or conventional bond? Evidence from Malaysian listed firms using partial adjustment models. *Pacific-Basin Finance Journal, 34*, 233–252.

Nasir, N.M., & Zainol, A. (2007). Globalisation of financial reporting: An Islamic focus. In: Godfrey, J.M., & Chalmers, K. (eds.), *Globalisation of Accounting Standards*. Cheltenham, UK: Edward Elgar, 261–274.

Pogue, T.F., & Soldofsky, R.M. (1969). What's in a bond rating? *Journal of Financial and Quantitative Analysis, 4*(2), 201–228.

Standard and Poor's. (2003). *Standard and Poor's Corporate Ratings Criteria*. New York: Standard and Poor's.

Usmani, M.T. (2002). *An Introduction to Islamic Finance*. Hague, Netherlands: Kluwer Law.

Usmani, M.T. (2007). Sukuk and their contemporary applications. AAOIFI Working Paper No n/a. Retrieved August 14, 2014, from www.ifseb.com/wpcontent/uploads/2012/07/Sukuk-and-Contemporary-application-14-JAN-08.pdf.

West, R.R. (1970). An alternative approach to predicting corporate bond ratings. *Journal of Accounting Research, 8*, 118–125.

White, H. (1980). A heteroskedasticity-consistent covariance matrix estimator and a direct test for heteroskedasticity. *Econometrica, 48*, 817–838.

Wibier, R.M., & Salah, O. (2011). The credit crunch and Islamic finance: Sharia-compliant finance against the backdrop of the credit crisis. *Journal of International Banking Law and Regulation, 26*, 509–515.

Wilson, R. (2008). Innovation in the structuring of Islamic Sukuk securities. *Humanomics, 24*, 170–181.

Chapter 6

Issuer's choice of Islamic bond type

Choice, the ultimate tragedy, the utmost honor, the savior of all miseries, and the beacon of all light. The power to choose not only gives strength but also exposes one to an eternal fear, that of regret. What if the choice turns out to be wrong? The decision requires the act of balancing and counterbalancing. The costs and the benefits are juxtaposed. Discovering the optimum turns into an addiction that causes one to strive and thrive. Islamic finance also offers a myriad of choices. The domain of the prohibited also offers freedom to choose. The pursuit of the desire for profit is subdued by the fear of risk. The dance of hope and fear gives birth to some Islamic financial products while offering the gift of annihilation to others.

6.1 Introduction

Various theories on capital structure seek to explain the optimal level of debt and equity for a firm. These theories contend that factors such as taxes, financial distress costs, and asymmetric information make the choice between debt and equity significant for an entity. Many studies have been conducted on the determinants of capital structure from a conventional financing perspective; however, in terms of the issuance of different types of Islamic financing, little research has been done. Do the conventional financing determinants of debt and equity have a similar impact on the different types of Islamic financing? One would indeed expect them to. Are there any other factors which affect the firm's choice of Islamic Sukuk with different debt and equity type features?[1]

The discussion in Chapter 5 focused on a particular model of Islamic financing, i.e., Sukuk. As mentioned, Sukuk are the Islamic counterpart to bonds and may be structured in many different ways. Some structures bear characteristics similar to debt while others are closer to equity. Broadly, the main types (discussed in the previous chapter) are Murabahah, Ijarah, and Musharakah Sukuk. The former two are comparable to debt while the latter is more closely aligned with equity. If this is indeed the case, one would expect the conventional capital structure determinants to have a similar impact in the case of these Islamic modes of financing. For example, firm-specific factors such as the leverage level, share prices, and profitability ratios have all been identified as factors which would influence an entity in terms of whether it chooses to raise funds through debt or equity. Furthermore, some studies identify additional factors which affect the choice of the type of debt issued (secured vs. unsecured, for example). This chapter seeks to identify the factors which affect the choice of Islamic bonds and explores whether these are similar to those identified in conventional financing studies.

6.2 Islamic bond structures

The three main types of Islamic Sukuk structures are Ijarah Sukuk, Murabahah Sukuk, and Musharakah Sukuk. The main characteristics of each of these are briefly discussed next.

6.2.1 Ijarah Sukuk

Ijarah Sukuk are normally issued by the firm through the creation of an independent Special Purpose Vehicle (SPV). The SPV issues the certificate to investors and raises the initial funds which are used to acquire the asset. Ownership of the asset rests with the Sukuk holders. The asset is leased to the issuing firm which is required to make rental payments for the Sukuk term. These cash flows are used to make payments to the investors periodically. At the end of the Sukuk term, the issuing firm purchases the asset at a pre-agreed price and these proceeds are passed on to the investors by the SPV.

6.2.2 Musharakah Sukuk

Musharakah (IJV) Sukuk structures allow investors to receive returns in accordance with the profit and loss sharing ratio. The SPV is used to issue Sukuk certificates and raise the initial funds which are then invested in a joint venture project with the issuing firm. The joint funds are used to acquire assets for use in the venture, and investors are paid a return periodically based upon the profit/loss generated by business. At maturity, all of the assets used in the venture are sold to the issuing firm at market value, and these proceeds are used to repay the Sukuk holders.

6.2.3 Murabahah Sukuk

Murabahah Sukuk are similar to a purchase on deferred payment terms arrangement. The SPV is again used to issue Sukuk certificates and raise the principal amount. This funding is used for the purchase of commodities which are then sold to the issuing firm on deferred payment terms. The periodic payments are used to pay the Sukuk holders their return for the duration of the Sukuk term.

6.3 Theories of capital structure

All corporate entities hold some level of debt and some level of equity. As with conventional financing, raising funds through Islamic instruments also falls into the two broad categories of equity and debt. The Musharakah bonds are similar to equity while Ijarah and Murabahah bonds are debt modes of financing. As mentioned earlier, determinants of Islamic modes of financing have not been extensively studied; however, some of the factors identified as determinants of conventional financing modes can potentially be extended to Islamic financing instruments. Different streams of literature provide contrasting explanations for what should be the optimal capital structure of a firm. Firms will generally satisfy their financing needs through some level of debt (borrowed funds, such as bank loans, debentures, bonds, etc.) and some level of equity (share capital and reserves). Both sources of funds have advantages and disadvantages. Since the leverage of a firm has a direct impact on its level of risk (generally speaking, greater borrowed funds result in greater risk) and its cost of capital, the capital structure choice will play a key role in determining the value of the firm. Hence, a key objective when making the capital structure decision is to balance the firm's financing needs with the need to simultaneously maximize shareholder wealth. This is not necessarily straightforward, since a number of conflicting factors come into play. Careful analysis is required to strike the most favorable balance between risk and return.

While the various capital structure theories argue that there is one particular optimal combination of debt versus equity financing which leads to the maximization of a firm's value, one of the earlier theories, developed by Modigliani and Miller in 1958, argued and proved that the debt-equity decision is irrelevant and has no impact on the cost of capital or on the valuation of the firm. The theory, however, was dependent upon the unrealistic assumption of perfect information (and assumed no taxes, no transaction costs, and no bankruptcy costs), and hence does not adequately model the state of affairs of the real world. Having said that, the intuition behind the theory has been appreciated, and modifications have subsequently followed allowing for the impact of taxation and other costs.

Another theory of capital structure, relevant in the context of imperfect information, is the trade-off theory. This states that each entity determines its optimal level of debt and equity by balancing off the relative costs and benefits of each. Trade-off theory incorporates the benefit of tax deductibility of debt against the increased risk of financial distress related to it. The trade-off theory states that the firm will incorporate some level of debt in its capital structure up to the point where the benefit of the tax shield is sufficient to offset the increase in the present value of the distress costs. Therefore, it suggests that firms with increased profitability are more likely to have higher debt ratios since they stand to benefit the most from this tax shield.[2] Tax deductibility of debt servicing costs makes Ijarah and Murabahah Sukuk more attractive, while financial distress costs—which are likely to be least for Musharakah Sukuk given their non-susceptibility to default—are likely to favor equity. Financial distress costs will result in increased risk and are considered to negatively affect the value of the firm. They include bankruptcy costs or the costs of reorganization. Agency costs may also be included here if there is a concern related to the creditworthiness of the organization.[3]

A further alternative explanation to the financing choice is offered through the pecking order theory which states that of the three modes of financing, namely internal, debt, and raising new equity, the most preferable is internal and the least preferable is equity. According to this explanation, asymmetric information affects the choice of financing of a firm. Managers—who are assumed to be better informed than investors about the true state of an organization—will prefer to avoid equity issues since these give a negative signal in the market that shares are overvalued.[4] Therefore, managers will initially prefer internal funds which can be raised without any negative signals. If internal funds are insufficient, then external funding is sought first through raising debt capital (with lesser negative signals) and then, as a last resort, through equity issuances. If this explanation is accepted, one would expect that profitable entities would not resort to external funds since their internal reserves should be sufficient.

A further extension of the above theories states that firms target a particular debt equity ratio and, when the actual differs from the target, it influences a firm in its financing choice so that the target level is achieved. Therefore, the debt-equity ratio of a firm is affected by the target ratio and factors which cause deviations from the target.

With regards to debt financing, conventional debt preferences may vary in terms of the seniority and security of the debt instrument. Literature has given conflicting explanations for the types of firms which would be more inclined toward secured debt as compared to unsecured debt. One strand states that high growth and highly levered firms are more likely to finance through secured debt,[5] while the opposite view argues that high-risk firms with limited growth opportunities are more likely to opt for secured finance since they would not be able to raise capital without offering security.[6]

6.3.1 Other possible factors

Other factors which might have a significant impact on the issuer's preference for the type of Islamic instrument include AAOIFI guidelines and Shariah advisor impact. Given that there are many different types of instruments, there is often conflict between different Shariah advisors as to whether the terms and conditions render the instrument Shariah compliant. Some instruments are approved by Shariah committees while others are approved by individual Shariah advisors. Those approved by committees are more likely to be considered Shariah compliant while the latter may be more prone to debate and scrutiny since they are dependent upon the viewpoint of one individual.

In terms of AAOIFI guidelines, the Shariah standards issued by AAOIFI provide strict rules as to what falls within acceptable Shariah boundaries and what falls beyond. The AAOIFI pronouncement in early 2008, stating that Musharakah Sukuk are not truly equity like in structure, was intended to ensure that future issuances should be compliant. It will be interesting to see if there is a pattern in terms of the Sukuk structures after the AAOIFI ruling. For example, did entities avoid IJV structures and move more toward Islamic debt bonds?

6.4 Implications for Islamic financing choices

Just as with conventional financing, intuitively the factors affecting the choice of debt or equity would be expected to have a similar impact on Islamic financing. Firm-specific factors such as profitability ratios and leverage levels as well as structural factors of the different instruments (i.e., whether they are structured to be more like debt or equity) are all likely to influence the choice of instrument. Furthermore, external events and the macroeconomic environment will also have an impact on the choice of financing.[7]

6.4.1 Factors affecting Musharakah issue

Musharakah Sukuk are similar in structure to equity since they are based on profit and loss sharing with no guarantees of returns. Based on the earlier theoretical discussion, some of the attributes of firms likely to favor Musharakah Sukuk might include an existing high level of leverage and share prices perceived to be overvalued. In a highly levered firm, it is likely that the current debt to equity ratio would be in excess of the target debt to equity ratio. Another implication is that firms with high existing levels of debt would face higher bankruptcy risk and thus would be less inclined to issue further debt and risk the possibility of adversely affecting the firm value. Therefore, a preference for equity type financing such as Musharakah Sukuk is likely to be high for firms in these scenarios. An examination of the data does not necessarily support this conclusion. Instead, it is seen that firms with a relatively higher proportion of long-term debt are more inclined toward Murabahah Sukuk whereas those with greater short-term debt favor Musharakah Sukuk. The results are not entirely intuitive. Nevertheless, a possible explanation for this scenario could be that Murabahah Sukuk generally have shorter maturities than Musharakah or Ijarah Sukuk, and, therefore, holding target debt to equity ratio constant, a higher long-term debt ratio should increase the issuer's propensity to issue Murabahah Sukuk. Another counter intuitive finding in relation to the issuance of Musharakah Sukuk is in respect of the valuation of shares. If a high market to book value ratio is indicative of overvalued stock, then the results do not suggest that a high ratio affects the issuer's preference for Musharakah Sukuk.

Some of the external factors expected to have an impact on the issuance of Musharakah Sukuk include the AAOIFI pronouncement of 2008 which dampened confidence in the Sukuk industry by declaring most Sukuk issuances were not Shariah compliant. Indeed, after 2008, there was a major slowdown in the industry, and Musharakah Sukuk are almost nonexistent to this date. The most likely reason for this could be the tougher and more stringent conditions imposed by AAOIFI in relation to bond structures to reflect their true risk-sharing nature.

6.4.2 Factors affecting Islamic debt (Murabahah or Ijarah) issue

Firms with a preference for debt as opposed to equity are likely to be large firms with high profitability, since they would generally have the ability to absorb the high interest costs. The data indeed suggest that high operating margin firms tend to opt for debt-based bonds. In terms of Ijarah Sukuk (which are the equivalent of secured debt), the theory leads us to believe that highly levered entities (which are riskier) would favor issuing Ijarah Sukuk as opposed to Murabahah Sukuk. However, this relationship is not necessarily evident in the results of the study, suggesting that not all Ijarah Sukuk represent actual ownership; although firms with higher bankruptcy risk did show a preference for Ijarah Sukuk.

6.5 Concluding remarks

This chapter discusses the determinants of different Islamic financing structures. The data suggest that Musharakah Sukuk are not considered to be equity replacements since their issuance is not affected by normal firm determinants of equity such as highly leveraged firms or overvalued share prices. As far as debt-based bonds are concerned, Ijarah bonds, which should represent ownership of the asset, should be perceived to be more secure than conventional secured debt; however, in reality, many bonds do not transfer ownership of the asset and hence are no different from secured conventional bonds. The conclusions have implications for regulators, Islamic bond issuers, and investors. For regulators, the visibility of less Shariah compliant structures becomes more apparent, and the need to bridge the gap becomes clear in order for the industry to grow and prosper. For investors as well as issuers, a closer scrutiny of instrument structures is needed since there appears to be a difference between actual and perceived structures.

Notes

1 The inspiration for the chapter comes from the paper by Azmat, Skully, and Brown (2014).
2 For further details, refer to Myers (2001).
3 Ibid.
4 For further details, refer to Myers and Majluf (1984).
5 For further details, refer to Stulz and Johnson (1985).
6 For further details, refer to Berger and Udell (1990).
7 Firm-specific, event-specific, and Islamic instrument-specific factors were tested by Azmat, Skully, and Brown (2014) in a study designed to explore the choice of Musharakah (IJV) bonds, Ijarah (SARA) bonds, and Murabahah (Islamic debt) bonds for 458 Malaysian corporate Islamic bond issues. The discussion following is based on the results of this study.

Bibliography

Azmat, S., Skully, M., & Brown, K. (2014). Issuer's choice of Islamic bond type. *Pacific-Basin Finance Journal, 28*, 122–135.

Berger, A., & Udell, G. (1990). Collateral, loan quality and bank risk. *Journal of Monetary Economics, 25*, 21–42.

Myers, S.C. (2001). Capital structure. *The Journal of Economic Perspectives, 15*(2), 81–102.

Myers, S.C., & Majluf, N.S. (1984). Corporate financing and investment decisions when firms have information that investors do not have. *Journal of Financial Economics, 13*, 187–221.

Stulz, R.M., & Johnson, H. (1985). An analysis of secured debt. *Journal of Financial Economics, 14*, 501–521.

Chapter 7

Risk in risk-sharing Sukuk

We cannot foresee the future so we settle for its predictions. Our ancient desire to see what is to come in a magic glass in an age of reason is now manifested in our beliefs in the outcome of sophisticated models. The purpose of models is to replace this simplification that we use to make any decisions, and to represent reality as a multitude of factors, their interactions in a dynamic setting with the ultimate objective to infer the probability of default. The model could never predict with certainty, unlike the seers of the past. Our model from the rational world could only give us a certain probability to the binary outcome that a default may occur.

7.1 Introduction

The market for credit risk models and the investors' need to follow their assessment emerge out of our primitive need for loss aversion. When losses hurt more than gains please, and the anticipation of losses is hurtful in equal measure, it makes sense to invest for the sake of security—no matter how false it may be. The upside of this sense of security is that it allows the investor to make efficient decisions, those that would ensure a good night's sleep, especially when the default event is far removed. Using these models for decision making also has a downside—they put the entire focus and attention of the investor on a singular aspect, the ability of the financial instrument (or the borrower) to return the money and not default. This model acts like a black box which absorbs an infinite amount of information but regurgitates a finite outcome with a common purpose—that of returning the principal. The rest of the information, no matter how valuable, is discarded. These models were specifically designed for debt instruments, where the objective of the instrument and the model serve each other well.[1]

7.2 Credit risk in risk-sharing bonds

With the advent of Islamic finance—and its desire to create financial instruments that can compete with conventional ones operating in a similar market and playing by the same rules—these Islamic finance instruments are required to have their credit risk measured. They need to be subjected to similar models of risk that can capture the default probability. This creates a familiar challenge of fitting a round peg in a square hole. The presence of credit risk models has a structural bias against Islamic finance instrument, especially those that have features of risk sharing. Islamic joint venture bonds with risk sharing features are different from conventional bonds. They share the upside of the firm's profits with the bond holder. In cases where the firm performs well and makes a substantial profit, this has to be shared with the Sukuk holders. The sharing of the upside comes at a price. In the case of loss, the issuer is under no compulsion to guarantee the principal. The issuer can pass the loss to the bond holder when the market value of the bond goes below the principal value. The bond holder has to bear the risk of the loss in coupon payments and a reduction in the bond's market value upon redemption.

Subjecting such a structure to credit risk models is a cause for concern. Intuitively speaking, by focusing entirely on the downside while ignoring the benefits the IJV structure offers on the upside, this creates a bias against them. The fact that the issuer can refuse coupon payment and the redemption value can be lower than the principal, increases the overall risk perception of the instrument, especially if conventional models of risk are used to gauge their suitability. It would be more appropriate to treat these instruments as equity, where we can use mean-variance to compensate the risk and the return when making decisions about them.

7.3 Structural credit risk models

Most structural models of credit risk are based on some core assumptions, the primary among them being the existence of a default boundary. Once the asset price hits this boundary, the default event occurs. The purpose of the structural model is simply to infer the probability of the asset price hitting the default boundary. These boundaries are varying in nature. The simplest models use the level of debt as the boundary and make advanced models that incorporate stochastic and random components. The random component adds precision to the probabilities, thus providing the necessary subtlety that it needs. To extend the credit risk models to Islamic instruments, first we need an artificial default boundary. Initially, Musharakah Sukuk do not have a default event as the issuer is under no compulsion to return the principal. As losses can be passed onto the issuer, the artificial default event would ensure that the Musharakah Sukuk holders are assured the principal with a random recovery rate.[2] If we measure the probability of default for the Musharakah structure using the artificial boundary, the credit models would provide an estimate of the default and an assessment of the bond credit risk. By focusing on the default event we ignore the upside of returns that the IJV structures are capable of offering. This would result in credit risk models assigning a higher risk and a lower rating to Islamic structures.

7.4 Concluding remarks

A possible reason why Musharakah might not have emerged in the market is due to their strong competition with conventional bonds, striving for the attention of investors who are interested in debt-like structures and use credit risk and ratings as the ultimate benchmark for their decisions. This puts the IJV structure at a significant disadvantage. When the conventional credit risk models are used to rate the structure which do not promise returning of the principal, the conventional risk models assign Islamic structures poor credit ratings as compared to conventional debt bonds. We propose that models used to measure risk and return of equity instruments should be used to evaluate IJV structures.

Notes

1 The inspiration for the chapter comes from the paper by Azmat, Skully, and Brown (2014).
2 For more details on the default boundary, see Azmat et al. (2016).

Bibliography

Acharya, V., & Naqvi, H. (2012). The seeds of a crisis: A theory of bank liquidity and risk taking over the business cycle. *Journal of Financial Economics*, *106*, 349–366.

Ammann, M. (2001). *Credit Risk Valuation: Methods, Models, and Applications*. 2nd ed. New York: Springer.

Ayub, M. (2007). *Understanding Islamic Finance*. Chichester, UK: John Wiley & Sons.

Azmat, S., Skully, M., & Brown, K. (2014). Credit risk in Islamic joint venture bond. *Journal of Economic Behavior & Organization*, *103*, S129–S145.

Azmat, S., Jalil, M.N., Skully, M., & Brown, K. (2016). Investor's choice of Shariah compliant 'replicas' and original Islamic instruments. *Journal of Economic Behavior & Organization*, *132*(supp), 4–22.

Benartzi, S., & Thaler, R. (1995). Myopic loss aversion and the equity premium puzzle. *The Quarterly Journal of Economics*, *110*, 73–92.

Black, F., & Cox, J.C. (1976). Valuing corporate securities: Some effects of bond indenture provisions. *Journal of Finance*, *31*, 351–367.

Blume, M.E., Lim, F., & MacKinlay, A.C. (1998). The declining credit quality of US corporate debt: Myth or reality? *Journal of Finance*, *53*, 1389–1413.

Bolton, P., Freixas, X., & Shapiro, J. (2012). The credit ratings game. *Journal of Finance*, *67*, 85–111.

Brennan, M.J., & Schwartz, E.S. (1980). Conditional predictions of bond prices and returns. *Journal of Finance*, *35*, 405–417.

Briys, E., & de Varenne, F. (1997). Valuing risky fixed rate debt: An extension. *The Journal of Financial and Quantitative Analysis*, *32*, 239–248.

Brunnermeier, M. (2009). Deciphering the liquidity and credit crunch 2007–08. *Journal of Economic Perspectives, 23*, 77–100.

Chong, B.S., & Liu, M.H. (2009). Islamic banking: Interest-free or interest-based? *Pacific-Basin Finance Journal, 17*, 125–144.

Duffie, D., & Singleton, K.J. (1999). Modelling term structures of defaultable bonds. *Review of Financial Studies, 12*, 687–720.

Duffie, D., & Singleton, K.J. (2003). *Credit Risk: Pricing, Management And Measurement.* Princeton, NJ: Princeton University Press.

EY. (2014). *World Islamic Banking Competitiveness Report 2013–14: The Transition Begins.* London: EY.

Finger, C.C., Finkelstein, V., Lardy, J.P., Pan, G., Ta, T., & Tierney, J. (2002). *CreditGrades Technical Document.* New York: RiskMetrics Group.

Howladar, K. (2006). *Shariah and Sukuk: A Moody's Primer (International Structured Finance Special Comment).* New York: Moody's Investors Service.

Jarrow, R.A., Lando, D., & Turnbull, S.M. (1997). A Markov model for the term structure of credit risk spreads. *Review of Financial Studies, 10*, 1–42.

Jarrow, R.A., & Turnbull, S.M. (1995). Pricing derivatives on financial securities subject to credit risk. *Journal of Finance, 50*, 53–85.

Kahneman, D., & Tversky, A. (1979). Prospect theory: An analysis of decision under risk. *Econometrica, 47*, 263–292.

Khan, F. (2010). How 'Islamic' is Islamic banking? *Journal of Economic Behavior & Organization, 76*, 805–820.

Lando, D. (2004). *Credit Risk Modelling: Theory and Applications.* Princeton, NJ: Princeton University Press.

Longstaff, F.A., & Schwartz, E.S. (1995). A simple approach to valuing risky fixed and floating rate debt. *Journal of Finance, 50*, 789–819.

Meissner, G. (2005). *Credit Derivatives: Application, Pricing, and Risk Management.* Malden, MA: Blackwell Publishing.

Merton, R.C. (1974). On the pricing of corporate debt: The risk structure of interest rates. *Journal of Finance, 29*, 449–470.

Standard and Poor's. (2003). *Standard and Poor's Corporate Ratings Criteria.* New York: Standard and Poor's.

Usmani, M.T. (2002). *An Introduction to Islamic Finance.* Hague, Netherlands: Kluwer Law International.

Usmani, M.T. (2007). *Sukuk and Their Contemporary Applications.* The Shariah Council.

Chapter 8

The challenge of Shariah compliance

The exchange of one thing for another provides a beautiful comfort, resulting in happiness for both the buyer and the seller. In the most detached of settings, in the absence of any emotional bond, it creates a relationship between two strangers where one serves the interest of the other. Price rather than proximity plays the role of the arbiter. The acceptance of price rather than person becomes paramount. The individual is secondary and the transaction is primary. Should everything be up for 'sale'? What about the matter involving the heart, where emotions precede economics, when even an iota of selfishness can contaminate the infinite goodness. What about matters of faith and religion? Should the spiritual be subdued to the rules of the material?

8.1 Introduction

The growth and prosperity of the Islamic finance industry stems from the needs of Shariah conscious investors and their demand for *halal* products. Why, then, do we see a multitude of products which are essentially replicas of conventional ones? This question is often posed by those skeptical about Islamic banking when they question the legitimacy of the discipline. Generally speaking, banks, financial institutions, and other instrument-issuing bodies are blamed for this situation. But is this a fair analysis, or does the investor also play a role? A detailed study of what has led to the extensive use of such replica structures is required: most importantly, who is the main driver of this phenomenon? This chapter explores this question in the context of a Sukuk-issuing firm and argues that in the presence of the agency problem between the firm and the investors, the profit maximization motive of the firm may lead to products which are *less* Shariah compliant (and hence more like replicas). This situation results in behavior which is contrary to the very spirit of Islamic banking. The following pages also discuss possible solutions to this problem.[1]

8.2 The complexity of Shariah compliant structures

Conventional bonds are debt contracts in which guaranteed return (interest) is paid to the bondholders over the term of the bond. At maturity, the bond is reacquired by the issuer at the face value. The element of predetermined returns in a debt contract means that such structures would not be considered Shariah compliant. Islamic bonds, therefore, contain many additional conditions and characteristics in order to be permissible under Islamic law. This clearly results in them incorporating greater levels of risk as compared to their conventional counterparts. For example, Sukuk entail considerable precision (and hence complexity) in terms of their structures. The issuing firm is required to create an independent SPV which is responsible for selling the Sukuk certificates and raising initial proceeds as well as acting as the intermediary for periodic payments to the investors. Therefore, many additional legal and transactional costs are associated with Islamic instruments. A further cost is that of obtaining approval from the Shariah scholar/committee who scrutinize the instrument particulars in detail to ensure that they do not violate any Shariah rulings.

8.3 The agency problem in Islamic banks

The agency problem refers to the situation which arises when there is a potential conflict of interest between two parties, even though one is expected to behave in the best interests of the other. In corporate finance, the agency problem is typically discussed in the context of shareholders (principal) and the management (agents) of the firm. There are many examples of situations where the latter may behave in a sub-optimal manner, i.e., this sub-optimal behavior results in an outcome which benefits the agent at the expense of the principal; for example, pursuing short-term profit goals for the purpose of a favorable bonus outcome at the expense of long-term benefits for shareholders. Much has been written about how the agency problem between shareholders and managers can be controlled. One possible solution is to give managers a shareholding in the firm. Another is the use of debt financing which forces outsiders (the lenders) to continuously monitor the entity and hence curb the possibility of sub-optimal decision making. The primary reason for the existence of this phenomenon is information asymmetry between the two parties, which allows agents to take decisions for their own benefit.

A similar situation can be inferred from the relationship between the profit-maximizing, Sukuk-issuing firm and its Shariah conscious investors. Here again, the predicament of information asymmetry gives rise to the possibility of one party acting in the pursuit of self-interest at the expense of the agent. The potential conflict here arises due to the classic trade-off between *cost* and *quality*. The primary concern for the issuing firm is profit maximization in which it looks for ways to reduce cost, for example by relaxing some of the stringent conditions of Shariah compliance (compromising on *quality*).

8.4 The Shariah certification dilemma

Most investors will inherently assume that the products offered meet Shariah requirements. The majority are unlikely to be exceptionally well versed in the detailed characteristics of the instrument. Instead, to neutralize the information asymmetry, they rely on the opinion of Shariah scholars (generally called Ulama). Shariah scholars—considered to be experts in Islamic law, especially with respect to provisions about finance—are advisors hired by the bank/issuing firm. They endorse or reject a product after a detailed evaluation of its structure to ensure compliance with Shariah principles. They issue a fatwa—a verdict on the Shariah compliance of a particular product—similar to an audit opinion issued by an auditor. Clearly, as far as a Shariah conscious investor is concerned, the fatwa holds great importance in terms of whether or not to invest in a particular product, since most investors are not experts in Islamic law themselves. Since all instruments are required to go through the rigorous process of examination by a Shariah scholar (or a committee) prior to being made available to the public, this Shariah certification will generally suffice for the customer.

However, there are some problems with placing extensive reliance on the Shariah advisor. Firms are able to disengage one particular advisor and hire another fairly easily if the fatwa is not favorable (this is particularly true for Islamic bonds, since bond issuing institutions do not have permanent scholars on board). This gives rise to the possibility of *fatwa shopping* where firms can go from advisor to advisor until they get the desired certification. Furthermore, Shariah advisors, due to this competition among themselves, may have an incentive to approve products which are less Shariah compliant. This collectively suggests that Islamic bonds which are not completely in conformity with Shariah regulations may be issued, particularly where the risk of getting caught through regulatory intervention is small.

8.5 The role of the regulator and Shariah conscious investor

In theory, this Shariah certification should be sufficient to satisfy the investors; however, in view of the competitive environment and profit-maximization objective, the issuing firm has an incentive to issue less compliant products with fewer costs associated with them. There are two possible solutions to deal with this. Firstly, the regulator needs to play a dominant role. Firms deviating from compliant structures should face a stiff penalty such that the incentive to do so is negated. Secondly, investors themselves need to step up and demand strictly Shariah compliant structures for which they are willing to bear the additional costs associated with them through a reduced Shariah premium. If both these factors are combined, there will be less incentive for issuing firms to offer less Shariah compliant products.

8.6 Concluding remarks

One outcome of the above discussion is that, in order for a firm to stay true to the spirit of Shariah principles and issue only pure Shariah compliant structures, there needs to be some sort of a penalty in place which offsets the potential benefit from noncompliance. Similarly, the potential long-term reputational loss and financial cost for the Shariah advisor for issuing an *incorrect* fatwa needs to be greater than the short-term financial gain of fees received. Therefore, the role of the regulator is critical. As with Islamic banks who have long-term relationships with their Shariah boards, perhaps a similar structure could be put in place for bond-issuing firms which disallows or discourages fatwa shopping. One possibility might be that a restriction be imposed that the first opinion issued by the advisor must be followed. As this alone will not completely rule out the possibility of *lenient* fatwas (since firms can choose advisors known to be lenient), there is also a need for similar restrictions to be placed on advisors; for example, random auditing with the risk of penalty where fatwas are not in conformity with Shariah principles.

The second key takeaway is that regulation alone is unlikely to be enough. Given the huge diversity in Shariah compliance for different products, countries, and Shariah advisors, ensuring uniformity in compliance is not easy. Therefore, there needs to be a strong Shariah conscious customer base that is willing to bear the higher cost associated with the product (through lower returns). Both the regulatory and ethical investor constraints will minimize the incentive of the profit-maximizing firm to deviate from Shariah compliance.

Note

1 The inspiration for the chapter comes from the paper by Azmat, Skully, and Brown (2014).

Bibliography

AAOIFI. (2008). Sukuk resolution. Retrieved June 13, 2009, from www.aaoifi.com/aaoifi_sb_sukuk_Feb2008_Eng.pdf.

Akerlof, G.A. (1970). The market for 'lemons': Quality uncertainty and the market mechanism. *Quarterly Journal of Economics*, *84*, 488–500.

Ali, S.S. (2005). *Islamic Capital Market Products: Developments and Challenges*. Research Paper No. 9. Jeddah, Saudi Arabia: Islamic Research and Training Institute, Islamic Development Bank.

Azmat, S., Skully, M., & Brown, K. (2014). The Shariah compliance challenge in Islamic bond markets. *Pacific-Basin Finance Journal, 28*, 47–57.

Beneish, M.D., & Press, E. (1993). Costs of technical violation of accounting-based debt covenants. *Accounting Review, 68*, 233–257.

Bester, H. (1985). Screening vs. rationing in credit markets with imperfect information. *American Economic Review, 75*, 850–855.

Bolton, P., Freixas, X., & Shapiro, J. (2012). The credit ratings game. *Journal of Finance, 67*, 85–111.

Chan, Y.S., & Thakor, A.V. (1987). Collateral and competitive equilibria with moral hazard and private information. *Journal of Finance, 42*, 345–363.

Chava, S., & Roberts, M.R. (2008). How does financing impact investment? The role of debt covenants. *Journal of Finance, 63*, 2085–2121.

Demiroglu, C., & James, C.M. (2010). The information content of bank loan covenants. *Review of Financial Studies, 23*, 3700–3737.

Diamond, D.W. (1984). Financial intermediation and delegated monitoring. *Review of Economic Studies, 51*, 393–414.

Diamond, D.W. (1989). Reputation acquisition in debt markets. *Journal of Political Economy, 97*, 828–862.

Edlin, A., & Stiglitz, J.E. (1995). Discouraging rivals: Managerial rent-seeking and economic inefficiencies. *American Economic Review, 85*, 1301–1312.

Felix, R. (2009). Islamic banks enjoy double-digit growth. *Khaleej Times*, November 7, accessed on May 17, 2018.

Freixas, X., & Rochet, J. (2008). *Microeconomics of Banking*. 2nd ed. London: MIT Press.

Hegazy, W. (2005). Fatwas and the fate of Islamic finance: A critique of the practice in contemporary Islamic financial markets. In: Nzain, A.S. (ed.), *Islamic Finance: Current Legal and Regulatory Issues*. Cambridge, MA: Islamic Finance Project, Harvard Law School, 133–149.

Jobst, A., Kunzel, P., Mills, P., & Sy, A. (2008). Islamic bond issuance: What sovereign debt managers need to know. *International Journal of Islamic and Middle Eastern Finance and Management, 1*, 330–344.

Kamali, M.H. (2005). The Islamic state: Origins, definitions and salient attributes. In: Nathan, K.S., & Kamali, M.H. (eds.), *Islam in South East Asia: Political, Social and Strategic Challenges for the 21st Century*. Singapore: Institute of Southeast Asian Studies, 278–300.

Leland, H., & Pyle, D. (1977). Informational asymmetries, financial structure and financial intermediation. *Journal of Finance, 32*, 371–387.

Malik, M.S., Malik, A., & Mustafa, W. (2011). Controversies that make Islamic banking controversial: An analysis of issues and challenges. *American Journal of Social and Management Sciences, 2*, 41–46.

Naim, A.M., Isad, M.Y., & Hamid, M.L. (2013). The effect of new AAOIFI standards on Sukuk in choosing the most authentic Islamic principles. *Journal of Islamic Accounting and Business Research, 4*, 77–93.

Nazim, A., & Bennie, G. (2012). *World Islamic Banking Competitiveness Report 2012–2013*. London: EY.

Ueda, M. (2004). Banks versus venture capital: Project evaluation, screening, and expropriation. *Journal of Finance*, *59*, 601–621.
Usmani, M.T. (2002). *An Introduction to Islamic Finance*. Hague, Netherlands: Kluwer Law International.
White, L.J. (2010). Markets: The credit rating agencies. *Journal of Economic Perspectives*, *24*, 211–226.

Chapter 9

Replicating conventional finance

The games we play define us. Some games are fair. They test our strength and resolve, manifesting the angelic side of our nature, turning even the losers into winners. The opportunity to play supersedes the ultimate victory. From the joy of competition sprouts the spring of glory. The lightness of being shrouds the heaviness of life. We recognize the essence of a thing by its opposite. The games of light are paid tribute to by the games of darkness. Where there exist no rules, or worst when the rules favor the side of the strong. These games manifest our worst nature. The destination pursued with greed devours the joy of the journey. The heaviness of being is the collateral damage. The credit rating games, started with the purest of intentions to level the playing field, have rigged our choices, with the originality of Islamic finance emerging as the ultimate sufferer.

9.1 Introduction

As the Islamic finance industry has emerged over the last few decades, the foremost need has been to provide a Shariah compliant alternative to conventional banking and investment products. The main target market has been the religiously conscious investor whose primary concern is to invest in 'halal' products. Although customers are clear in their objective to invest in Islamic products, it can be safely said that few fully understand the core principles of Islamic economics and the 'why' behind the structuring of the products. By and large, they place their trust in the certification from the Shariah advisor. Indeed, many customers lack even the most basic understanding of some of the fundamental questions such as why is Riba prohibited, or why even the principal amount is not guaranteed? These questions are concerned with the core principles of Islamic banking and form the cornerstone of the subject. The story of the poor man, narrated at the start of the book, who had to borrow at an extortionate rate to fund a wedding, and that of the astute businessman who wanted to borrow to fund a sure shot successful business proposition, help us answer these questions. In a nutshell, any sorts of *guarantees* in a loan are prohibited in

Islamic law because they ultimately result in injustice and inequity in the distribution of wealth. It is not fair on the borrower to be charged exorbitant rates of interest. Similarly, it is equally unfair and inequitable if the lender is paid less than the due share for funding a highly successful business venture. Why should the lender not receive an amount in proportion to the success of the project? Therefore, not only do Islamic economic principles cater for injustice toward the borrower but also toward the lender. This results in the philosophy of risk sharing which is an integral part of Islamic finance. So much so that there is a general agreement among scholars that 'risk-sharing' products are the 'true' Islamic alternative to conventional products. The Islamic investor accepts that there are no guarantees that she would earn any return or even that her principal investment will be assured. Compared to the mainstream traditional banking models, this is clearly a far riskier proposition for investors and poles apart from what they are used to. However, it has been accepted due to religious preferences. Despite the importance of risk sharing, the growth of the industry over the past few years has not witnessed the surge in risk-sharing products which was anticipated.[1]

Depositors and investors, who were tuned to a particular (less risky) model of banking, needed to be gently eased into this new mindset; even those who were religiously sensitive. Safer alternatives to the risk-sharing model were sought. Products were often *tweaked* so that they did not fully share the risk with the investor. One such example is evident in the Sukuk industry. The 2008 AAOIFI pronouncement that most Sukuk issuances where declared non Shariah compliant was a stark eye opener. The key objections related directly to the risk-sharing philosophy and how it had been compromised; for example, the fact that many Sukuk were not resulting in a real transfer of ownership of the underlying asset to the Sukuk holder. Also, the guarantee of the Musharakah Sukuk-issuing firm to return the principal was declared incorrect. The makeshift strategy intended to introduce the risk-sharing mindset to a risk-averse customer base appears to have backfired, with product structures often questioned as actually crossing the boundaries of Shariah compliance.

Other Shariah compliant *alternatives* to the risk-sharing model have continued to be introduced to boost the industry and provide a 'stepping stone' between conventional and Islamic products. As a result, the religiously conscious investors now have a choice. They could opt for either high- or low-risk products based upon their own risk appetites but with the peace of mind that these were Shariah compliant. When investors are given a choice of Shariah compliant instruments, behavioral considerations suggest that the less risky alternative is likely to prevail.

Despite strongly advocating risk sharing as the 'Islamic' way forward, even the Islamic investor did not appear to be fully prepared for it. This chapter looks at this aspect of Islamic capital markets (ICMs) more closely to try to understand why Islamic debt bonds and Islamic equities are the dominant feature in ICMs and why risk-sharing Musharakah is almost nonexistent.

9.2 Instrument structures

Details of the main Sukuk structures are given in Chapter 5 (refer to Section 5.1). Broadly speaking, one may classify Ijarah Sukuk and Murabahah Sukuk as debt based since there is no element of risk sharing involved and returns are fixed. A Musharakah Sukuk, however, operates in a profit and loss sharing manner. Sukuk holders receive periodic returns based upon the profit and loss sharing ratio. Profit sharing ratios are predetermined whereas losses are shared in proportion to the investment made (a necessary requirement for Shariah compliance). Islamic equities refer to a restricted list of equities approved by the Shariah board of entities engaging in Shariah compliant businesses and transactions. Any activities considered un-Islamic, such as alcohol trade, would disqualify the entities from falling under the Islamic equities category. Islamic equities are therefore another viable investment option for Shariah conscious investors.

9.3 Behavioral explanations

Economic theory quite intuitively suggests that a utility maximizing individual should invest in financial instruments which maximize her utility. The nature of the investor's loss aversion would clearly impact the investment portfolio with highly loss-averse investors opting for less risky financial instruments with stable returns. Debt-based instruments, therefore, emerge as the obvious choice. Murabahah Sukuk may be a far safer proposition for risk-averse investors; however, equity- or Musharakah-based Sukuk are expected to generate higher returns. This is supported by empirical evidence dating back to the 19th century which strongly suggests that equity provides a significantly greater return than debt over the long term. This phenomenon has been branded the *equity premium puzzle*. Benartzi and Thaler (1995) determined that for the US market since 1926, the annual returns from equity stood at around 7% while the real return from treasury bills in the same period was less than 1%. What has puzzled economists is the size of the premium, which is so large that it cannot simply be explained by risk aversion (Mehra & Prescott, 1985). In fact, in the same paper, the authors refer to another study in which it was found that risk aversion must be in the region of 30 to explain the magnitude of the premium, whereas it actually stands at 1 to 2. Attempts to understand this puzzle have triggered many studies questioning why the premium is so large and why investors would want to hold any debt in this scenario.

One such explanation emanating from a behavioral angle is that although investors would always aim to maximize their returns, they are more sensitive to losses than they are to gains. This is known as *myopic loss aversion*.[2] Therefore, they are willing to forego higher gains due to the higher risks. In the short term, returns from equity have been shown to be far more volatile than from debt. Accordingly, investors who are loss averse and frequently (at least once a year) evaluate their investments are more likely to prefer debt due to the unpredictability of equity returns in the short term. This type of behavior suggests that investors with a short-term planning horizon have a higher utility from debt than from equity, and similarly those with a longer planning horizon will prefer risk-sharing-type investments like equity or Musharakah.

9.4 Implications for investor preferences

For a profit-maximizing firm seeking to raise funds, the objective is always to issue those instruments which offer minimal returns to investors. For the Shariah compliant investor, adherence to Shariah principles is a significant component of utility maximization. Where the choice is between a risky Shariah compliant instrument and a less risky non Shariah compliant instrument, the investor should opt for the former choice. However, given the option to choose among various Shariah compliant instruments, emphasis may shift back to their risk return status when making a decision.

Behavioral irrationalities such as myopic loss aversion suggest that the investor must negotiate a significantly high profit rate from Musharakah instruments (which is done *ex-ante* and is not changeable during the life of the instrument) in order that her utility from investing in a Musharakah is greater than or equal to the alternatives. Since the returns are likely to differ in the short term and the long term, the investor's evaluation period plays a key role. For a short evaluation period in which risk-sharing options are likely to give more volatile returns and generate lower investor utility, Murabahah Sukuk should crowd out the risk-sharing alternatives. For longer evaluation periods in which equity and risk-sharing returns are higher than debt instruments, the investor's utility from such instruments will exceed debt and these will hence become the preferred options.

As far as Islamic equities and Musharakah are concerned, they share similar features on the loss side since losses are proportional to the investments. However, on the profit side, returns can differ since Musharakah returns are negotiated in advance and can vary from the loss ratio. Equity can therefore be considered a special form of Musharakah, where the profit and loss sharing rates are equal. In the choice between the two instruments, a profit-maximizing firm would prefer a Musharakah instrument to equity, only if the expected return it pays investors is lower than the expected return on equity. However, since the profit rate is negotiated at the outset, the return on Musharakah and its associated utility can be either greater or less than that of Islamic equities in the short term. For longer evaluation periods, the returns from both instruments are expected to converge.

When comparing Islamic equities with Musharakah, one would not expect a significant difference in the utilities of the two types of instruments since both are risk sharing in nature and with a similar structure. However, in a study conducted by Azmat, Jalil, Skully, and Brown (2016),[3] the investor utilities of both instruments were graphed and compared. The graphs revealed that for evaluation periods of more than six months, the investor's utility from equities is greater than or equal to that from Musharakah. For shorter periods, however, Musharakah utility is marginally better than equity. This suggests that for longer evaluation periods (exceeding six months), Islamic equities crowd out Musharakah.

9.5 Concluding remarks

This discussion began by identifying certain behavioral irrationalities such as myopic loss aversion in an effort to understand and explain why Islamic capital markets are dominated by debt bonds and Islamic equities. The results suggest that Islamic bonds are the preferred choice of investors with a shorter evaluation period while Islamic equities are preferable over longer evaluation periods. These findings question the 'stepping stone' strategy where certain Islamic products that are similar to conventional products are approved, with the assumption that they would help promote the eventual emergence of the original, truly Islamic instruments like Musharakah. In fact, it would appear that these products have hindered and crowded out Islamic structures rather than facilitating them.

Notes

1 The inspiration for the chapter comes from the paper by Azmat et al. (2016).
2 Refer to Benartzi and Thaler (1995) for a more detailed explanation.
3 Azmat et al. (2016).

Bibliography

Azmat, S., Jalil, M.N., Skully, M., & Brown, K. (2016). Investor's choice of Shariah compliant 'replicas' and original Islamic instruments. *Journal of Economic Behavior & Organization*, *132*(supp), 4–22.

Benartzi, S., & Thaler, R.H. (1995). Myopic loss aversion and the equity premium puzzle. *Quarterly Journal of Economics*, *110*, 73–92.

Mehra, R., & Prescott, E. (1985). The equity premium puzzle. *Journal of Monetary Economics*, *15*(1985), 145–161.

Chapter 10

Can Islamic banks have their own benchmark?

'Sometimes you get an insight in the most unlikely of places during unexpected circumstances. Some years ago I had one such experience. I was invited by an Islamic banker for a meeting, someone who had seen the field develop and blossom since its inception. He had seen it all, the zeal of its founders, the critique of the opponents, and the jealousy of friends. The success of the Islamic finance industry, both the sudden and the subtle, had far exceeded his expectations, though not so much his desires. He had reached an age where the last signs of vitality were dissipating quickly, while the first signs of old age had begun to manifest. It was not so much the age but the years spent in the competitive environment that had taken its toll. Witnessing the worst of human nature, the betrayals, the lies, the hypocrisies and deceptions, the feeling of trust seemed most alienated, replace conveniently with skepticism. The years had made him cold, the simple emotions seemed most ludicrous. Solace could only be found with God and so he did. He was fasting that day, sacrificing his desires for the ultimate reality. I walked into his office, a well decorated one with some apparent indulgences. He greeted me with respect, though the implicit detachment and the absence of warmth were obvious. The initial exchange of pleasantries made apparent his impatience; there was much on his mind with time as the obvious betrayer. I started asking him about his success and the institution that he had built. His response was perplexing and amusing'.

'Well! We do not sit in the ivory tower'.

It was a snide remark aimed at the ideals that academicians hold, what men of practice seem most devoid of. It was also a defense mechanism, to hide the inner insecurity in the face of the staunch criticism that bankers have to face from academicians. The distinction between the ivory tower thinking and the practical actions have divided many another field. Probably Islamic finance has suffered more so, for the wedge between its ideals and actions is most significant. It seems most ironical that the industry that was built on lofty ideals considers the principles of its founding fathers a burden, something to be avoided rather than embraced. Sensing my disapproval of his stream of thinking, he quickly turned to certain facts about the industry, a justification for why the ideals and reality are most segregated. He said:

'Ten percent of our customers are driven by a faith so strong that they would never think of switching away from Islamic banking. Ten percent of the customers in the market are averse to religion to the extent they would never switch from conventional banking. The remaining 80% are indifferent and make their decisions on the basis of who could offer the most lucrative rates and the best services'.

As a good businessman, he believed in the sovereignty of the customer. He attributed his success to understanding his customers and acting in accordance with their pleasure. It is easy to forget that, at the end of the day Islamic banks, like any other business, are in the market to make money. The idealism of the industry is contingent on the idealism of the customers.

10.1 Introduction

One of the key objections raised by those opposing Islamic finance is that the benchmark rate used for Islamic financial products is based on the conventional interbank rate.[1] Islamic and conventional banks worldwide use a common interbank offer rate for the pricing of their instruments. This puts into question the religiosity of the underlying structures, which are based on a Riba-free and risk-sharing ideology. Being a nascent industry, the use of conventional rates to price its products was not intended to be a long-term solution; however, as a stepping stone strategy in the absence of other alternatives, it was considered acceptable by Shariah scholars until an Islamic benchmark rate was created. This situation gave rise to two strongly opposing schools of thought. One extreme argued that any connection with forbidden interest rates was contrary to the principles of the Islamic economic system. If the underlying pricing strategy was unfair and unjust, how could the final outcome lead to distributive justice? In order for this to be achieved, the benchmark should be based on the actual performance of real assets in conformity with Shariah guidelines.[2] On the other side, it was argued that the use of interest-based benchmarks by Islamic financial institutions was permissible from a Shariah perspective and did not render the underlying transaction invalid.[3]

In any case, it was always envisaged that the Islamic banking industry would in due course, once it had grown to a significant size, create its own mechanism for the pricing of its unique set of products which would have a risk profile distinct from its conventional counterparts. The Islamic rate would (or should) be independent of the conventional rate.[4] The first such effort for a separate profit-based rate for the Islamic finance industry came in 2011. Thomson Reuters began the initiative of calculating an Islamic interbank rate as the much-awaited alternative to the conventional benchmark. Known as the Islamic interbank benchmark rate (IIBR), it is based on the contributions of 18 Middle Eastern Islamic banks and fully segregated Islamic windows and is intended as an indicator of the risk profile of Islamic products and services. The launch of its own independent benchmark is viewed as a key milestone for the industry; however, IIBR is still not universally used across the industry. In fact, the industry predominantly continues to rely on conventional benchmarks, and, to date, only a limited number of banks and financial institutions have priced their products based on IIBR.

This chapter looks at whether this initiative for an independent Islamic rate has been successful and also investigates the extent to which this has contributed to the credibility of the Islamic finance industry. Have the negative perceptions associated with a conventional rate been overcome? The methodology for the determination of IIBR and LIBOR (London Interbank Offered Rate) is discussed, and the relationship between the resultant rates is studied to establish the extent to which they are decoupled from one another. The reasons for the differences between the two benchmark rates (the IIBR-LIBOR spread) is also investigated.

10.2 Islamic interbank benchmark rate (IIBR)

In 2011, the initiative for an Islamic benchmark rate was started by a consortium of 18 Islamic Middle Eastern banks and windows as an objective and independent indicator of the average cost of funding short-term interbank Shariah compliant funding transactions. The goal was to break away from the shadow of the conventional rate which had created considerable criticism for the industry. However, although IIBR is approved by Shariah scholars, it is still not widely followed.

Various organizations collaborated in order to make this venture possible, including the Islamic Development Bank (IDB), Accounting and Auditing Organisation of Islamic Financial Institutions (AAOIFI), the Bahrain Association of Banks (BAB), and Hawkamah Institute for Corporate Governance,[5] together with Thomson Reuters who are also responsible for various other famous benchmarks including the LIBOR and EURIBOR.[6] Thomson Reuters calculates and publishes the rates on a daily basis.

The procedure for fixing and announcing IIBR is illustrated in Figure 10.1. The final rate fixing of IIBR is guided by two independent committees: the Shariah Committee and the Islamic Benchmark Committee. The former is responsible for ensuring that IIBR complies with Shariah principles, while the latter provides commercial and technical advice required for the proper implementation and on-going integrity of IIBR. The Islamic Benchmark Committee is also responsible for selecting, admitting, and excluding banks to the contributor panel. The involvement of these numerous bodies reinforces the strong governance structure and gives weight to the legitimacy of the process for deriving the Islamic benchmark.

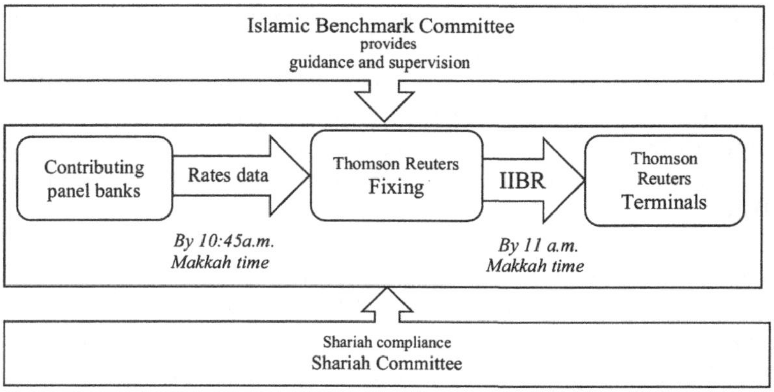

Figure 10.1 Procedure for fixing and final publication of IIBR (Azad et al., 2018, 8)[7]

10.2.1 Methodology for deriving IIBR

The process for the calculation of the daily IIBR begins with the contributor panel forwarding their rates for Shariah compliant US dollar (USD) funding of a reasonable market size to Thomson Reuters between 9:00 a.m. and 10:44 a.m., Makkah time (GMT+3). The rates are forwarded based on a pre-defined question which is put forth by the IBC and approved by the Shariah Committee. At 10:45 a.m., Thomson Reuters takes the rates forwarded and performs its own audit and review procedures to ensure that the rates contributed are genuine. The rates are ranked from highest to lowest before removing the top and bottom quartiles (25%) to eliminate the effect of outliers. This effectively leaves eight rates for the calculation of IIBR, and their mean average (rounded to five decimal places) results in the IIBR figure. This is made public at 11:00 a.m., Makkah time.

10.2.2 Methodology for deriving LIBOR

Since February 1, 2014, Intercontinental Exchange Benchmark Administration Limited has taken over the administration of LIBOR, changing it to the ICE LIBOR. LIBOR is fixed each day between 11:10 a.m. and 11:59:59 a.m., London time. The rate is used to provide a basis for calculating the short-term interest rates globally. It is also the benchmark rate used for the settlement of interest rate contracts on many of the major futures and options exchanges around the world. There are a number of steps carried out to calculate the final rate. Firstly, the contributing panel members are each required to supply a rate shortly before 11:00 a.m. each business day. The ICE LIBOR submissions are based on the following question: ‘At what rate could you borrow funds, were you to do so by asking for and then accepting interbank offers in a reasonable market size just prior to 11 am London time?' The submissions forwarded are based upon the lowest perceived rate at which a bank could go into the London interbank money market and obtain funding of reasonable market size, for a given maturity and currency. Once all submissions are received, the next step is to rank the rates and exclude the top and bottom quartiles. The mid two quartiles are then arithmetically averaged and the result is rounded to five decimal places to create an ICE LIBOR rate, which is made public at 11:00 a.m. GMT. This process is repeated for every currency and maturity, producing 35 rates every business day.[8]

10.3 IIBR-LIBOR benchmark rates and convergence

Figure 10.2 shows the daily six-month IIBR and LIBOR rates in percentage points, both in USD for the period from November 14, 2011, through October 9, 2015. Figure 10.2 shows that IIBR is consistently above LIBOR in this period (except for the initial period until April 2011, in which there was an error in the calculation of the rate).

It is well understood that the distinguishing feature of Islamic finance is the absence of guaranteed returns on debt. Riba is defined as the predetermined excess to the principal in a loan contract. The industry overcame this prohibition by developing products which ensured that either or both of the contentious points were removed from a transaction, i.e., the *predetermined excess* element and/or the *loan contract* element. This, therefore, gave rise to risk-sharing instruments, such as Musharakah and Mudarabah, or asset-based instruments, such as Murabahah and Ijarah. The pricing of these products was initially based on conventional benchmarks to encourage growth in a highly competitive environment. The industry has certainly thrived and today is seen as a rapidly growing global phenomenon. However, it still represents only a fraction of the total finance world. Changes in the terminology and jargon have created a perception of difference; yet, in finance terms, their underlying risk is considered by many to be similar to conventional finance. Accordingly, given the similarity in the risk profile, the pricing of the Shariah compliant products can largely be seen to converge with conventional instruments. Any attempt to price the products differently is therefore unlikely to succeed due to the relatively small size of the industry, the competitive environment, and arbitrage.

From Figure 10.2, IIBR is clearly seen to have a higher mean average than LIBOR. The movement of the two benchmarks is further analyzed by Azad et al. (2011) using various tests to confirm their short- and long-term relationship.[9] The results indicate a highly positive correlation for the entire sample period. This suggests that both rates co-move and that the spread is highly persistent. Furthermore, the two rates are co-integrated, and there is indeed a long-term equilibrium relationship between them for all maturities.

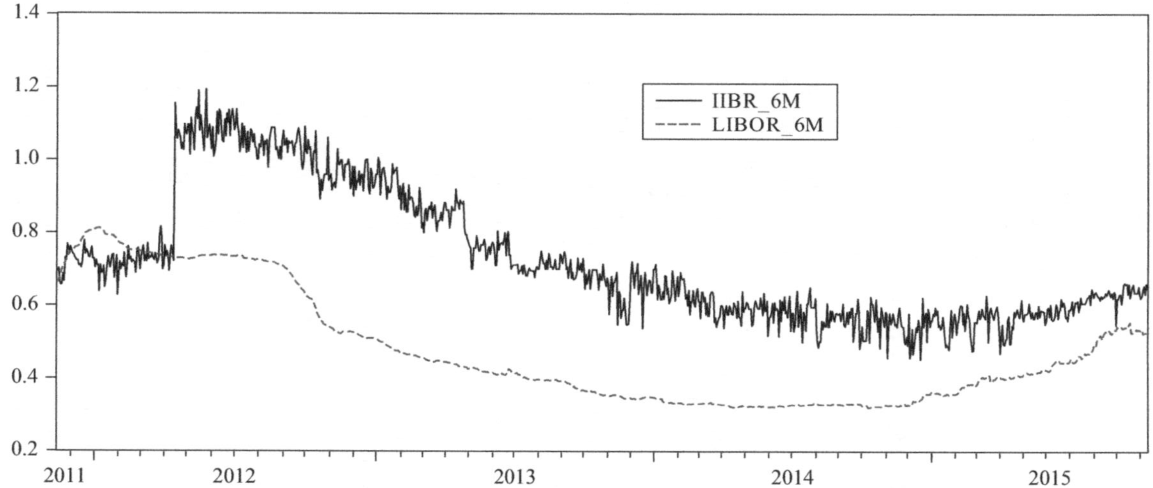

Figure 10.2 IIBR-LIBOR rates (six months) (Graph from Azmat et al., 2015, 5)

Thus the spread between IIBR and LIBOR is expected to be stable, with the Islamic banks' lending rate being consistently higher than LIBOR. This represents a 'piety premium' which the borrowing banks are willing to pay the lending (Islamic) banks for providing Shariah compliant funding.

10.4 Determinants of the 'piety premium'

Figure 10.2 shows that throughout the period under study, IIBR is consistently higher than its conventional counterpart. Various studies (conducted in the context of conventional benchmarks) have suggested a number of different factors which impact upon the credit spreads of the two interbank benchmark rates. The intrinsic bank risk and various market wide factors are thought to be key determinants.[10] Specifically, factors such as the treasury rate, the slope of the yield curve, changes (and volatility) in the stock price of panel banks, as well as their credit ratings,[11] are all thought to play a role in influencing the spread of different benchmark rates. While these studies explore conventional rate spreads, similar inferences could be drawn when exploring the IIBR-LIBOR spread. Some of these factors are discussed in more detail later. The discussion is useful for the various and diverse stakeholders, e.g., regulators, investors, banks, central banks of the panel bank countries, and those institutions responsible for the IIBR benchmark setting.

10.4.1 Treasury rate and yield curve

The treasury rate is said to negatively impact the interest rate spread for conventional banks. This was found in a study conducted to investigate the TIBOR-LIBOR spread (TIBOR is the Tokyo interbank offered rate).[12] Where deposit rates are reasonably rigid, any increase in the lending rates of banks will directly impact the profit and reduce the default risk. Although for Islamic banks any increase in the profits of the bank must be shared with deposit holders, similar, albeit somewhat less significant, inferences can be drawn for Islamic banks.

The yield curve, which depicts the return on bonds of different maturities, is used by analysts as an indicator of future economic activity. Typically, the difference between the yields for the two-year and ten-year maturities are compared and the slope of the resultant graph provides insights on various economic indicators such as interest rates, inflation, and also overall economic growth.

The *normal* shape for the graph is upward sloping since a higher yield is expected for bonds of longer maturities while a lower yield would be expected for shorter-term bonds. However, fluctuating rates mean that the slope is continuously changing in terms of the steepness of its gradient or even, in extreme cases, a negative gradient. When the difference between the long-term and short-term bonds is large, the curve is steeper, and when the difference reduces, the curve becomes flatter. A steep curve suggests that investors are demanding higher long-term rates, which is often seen as an indicator of a future increase in inflation and stronger future economic growth. Thus a higher return is demanded by investors as maturities are extended to compensate for the risk of loss in value associated with higher inflation. However, when inflation is not a key concern, the difference shrinks and the curve flattens. A steeper slope is also thought to reflect the anticipation of financial markets of future increases in short-term interest rates (to counter the increased inflation). This will lead to a reduction in the bank's default probability thus reducing the IIBR-LIBOR spread.[13]

10.4.2 Stock prices of contributing panel banks

The contrasting feature of Islamic banks is that they do not offer fixed returns on their deposits. The return paid to depositors varies in accordance with the profit earned by the bank. A higher profit means that customers receive higher returns while the same is true in reverse. Furthermore, the risk-sharing nature of all instruments means that the principal amount of the deposit is also not guaranteed and depositors can be refused withdrawals. This entire structure can be compared to the relationship between shareholders and the corporation. Shareholders receive no guarantees in respect of the principal investment or the dividend payout. However, the dividend paid is dependent upon the profit earned by the enterprise. Depositors of Islamic banks are therefore similar to equity participants. They will continue to invest as long as the marginal productivity equals the marginal cost of capital. The IIBR rate (which is a reflection of the industry's riskiness) should therefore reflect the cost of funding and profit potential of the participating Islamic banks.

A higher profit potential of a participating panel bank, which is reflected in a higher stock price, indicates a strong outlook and reduced risk of default. This should therefore reduce the spread. Greater volatility of the stock price index, on the other hand, suggests greater risk and hence a higher premium. This argument holds stronger for Islamic banks, which are based on the equity participation model and where stock prices and their volatility will have a direct impact on the profitability of the bank. For conventional banks, there is no causal relationship between the bank's profit and the interest paid. It therefore follows that increasing stock prices should have a negative impact on the spread, while greater volatility of the stock price index is likely to increase it.

10.4.3 Credit ratings

For conventional banks, positive market news and credit ratings for a panel bank would be expected to have a negative impact on the Interbank spread[14] between two banks, due to lower perceived risk and improved profitability prospects. Similarly, bad news and lower ratings would have the opposite impact. As far as Islamic banks are concerned, this argument can be extended to suggest that in a competitive market, good news or improved credit ratings strengthen the position of the bank to charge a higher Shariah premium, thus increasing the spread. Bad news would have the opposite impact.

10.5 Concluding remarks

The Islamic banking industry is operating in an environment dominated by conventional players. Furthermore, the risk profile of Islamic products and services is more or less comparable to those of conventional banks. Against this background, it is highly unlikely that the Islamic benchmark rate can be isolated completely from the conventional global benchmark rate. The rates will always converge regardless of the size of the industry unless the product offerings of Islamic banks become significantly distinct—structurally—from conventional ones. The stability of the spread between IIBR and LIBOR, referred to as the 'piety premium', may exist and can be attributed to the unique risk of Islamic banks. The co-integration of the two rates and the stability of the spread, however, suggest that the effort to create an independent benchmark for the industry has not been successful. A truly decoupled and independent benchmark for the Islamic banking industry can only become a reality if the products are structured to be visibly distinct and decoupled from their conventional counterparts.

Notes

1 For further details, please refer to one example of such a study by Azad et al. (2018). The arguments presented in this chapter are inspired by this paper.
2 For further details, refer to Choudhury (2011).
3 For further details, refer to Usmani (2002).
4 For further details, refer to Khan (2010).
5 www.thomsonreuters.com/content/dam/openweb/documents/pdf/tr-com-financial/fact-sheet/iibr.pdf, retrieved March 7, 2018.
6 www.thomsonreuters.com/content/dam/openweb/documents/pdf/tr-com-financial/fact-sheet/iibr.pdf, retrieved March 7, 2018.
7 Thomson Reuters (www.financial.thomsonreuters.com/islamicbenchmark).
8 www.theice.com/iba/libor#calculating, retrieved March 8, 2018.
9 The long-term equilibrium relationship is tested using Johansen cointegration tests while the short-term dynamic relationship is established using the dynamic conditional correlation (DCC) model of Engle (2002).
10 For further details, refer to Longstaff and Schwartz (1995).
11 For further details, refer to Covrig et al. (2004).
12 Ibid.
13 Ibid.
14 Ibid.

Bibliography

AAOIFI, 2008. Sukuk resolution. Retrieved June 13, 2009, from www.aaoifi.com/aaoifi_sb_sukuk_Feb2008_Eng.pdf.

Ayub, M. (2007). *Understanding Islamic Finance*. Chichester, UK: John Wiley & Sons.

Azad, A.S.M.S., Azmat, S., Chazi, A., & Ahsan, A. (2018). Can Islamic banks have their own benchmark? *Emerging Markets Review*, (In press). doi: 10.1016/j.ememar.2018.02.002.

Azad, A.S.M.S., Fang, V., & Wickramanayake, J. (2011). Low-frequency volatility of yen interest rate swap market in relation to macroeconomic risk. *International Review of Finance*, *11*(3), 353–390.

Azmat, S., Skully, M., & Brown, K. (2015). Can Islamic banking ever become Islamic? *Pacific-Basin Finance Journal*, *34*, 253–272.

Azmat, S., Jalil, M.N., Skully, M., & Brown, K. (2016). Investor's choice of Shariah compliant 'replicas' and original Islamic instruments. *Journal of Economic Behavior & Organization*, *132*(supp), 4–22.

Beck, T., Demirgüç-Kunt, A., & Merrouche, O. (2013). Islamic vs. conventional banking: Business model, efficiency and stability. *Journal of Banking & Finance*, *37*(2), 433–447.

Bedendo, M., Cathcart, L., & El-Jahel, L. (2007). The shape of the term structure of credit spreads: An empirical investigation. *Journal of Financial Research*, *30*(2), 237–257.

Blanco, R., Brennan, S., & Marsh, I.W. (2005). An empirical analysis of the dynamic relation between investment-grade bonds and credit default swaps. *Journal of Finance*, *60*(5), 2255–2281.

Chong, B.S., & Liu, M.-H. (2009). Islamic banking: Interest-free or interest-based? *Pacific-Basin Finance Journal*, *17*(1), 125–144.

Choudhury, M.A. (2011). Islamic economics and finance: An epistemological inquiry. In: Baltagi, B.H., Sadka, E., & Choudhury, M.A. (eds.), *Contributions to Economic Analysis* 291. Bingley, UK: Emerald.

Churm, R., & Panigirtzoglou, N. (2005). Decomposing credit spreads. Bank of England Working Paper no # 253. Bank of England, Threadneedle Street, London, EC2R 8AH.

Collin-Dufresne, P., Goldstein, R.S., & Martin, J. S. (2001). The determinants of credit spread changes. *Journal of Finance*, *56*(6), 2177–2207.

Covrig, V., Low, B.S., & Melvin, M. (2004). A yen is not a yen: Tibor/Libor and the determinants of the Japan premium. *Journal of Financial & Quantitative Analysis*, *39*(1), 193–208.

Engle, R. (2002). Dynamic conditional correlation: A simple class of multivariate generalized autoregressive conditional heteroskedasticity models. *Journal of Business & Economic Statistics*, *20*(3), 339–350.

Khan, F. (2010). How 'Islamic' is Islamic banking? *Journal of Economic Behavior & Organization*, *76*(3), 805–820.

Longstaff, F.A., & Schwartz, E.S. (1995). A simple approach to valuing risky fixed and floating rate debt. *The Journal of Finance*, *50*(3), 789–819.

Merton, R.C. (1974). On the pricing of corporate debt: The risk structure of interest rates. *Journal of Finance*, *29*(2), 449–470.

Reuters, T. (2011). Islamic interbank benchmark rate faq. Retrieved December 17, 2012, from www.sesric.org/imgs/news/image/646-faq.pdf.

Reuters, T. (2013a). State of the global Islamic economy report. Retrieved March 11, 2014, from www.iedcdubai.ae/assets/uploads/files/tr-state-of-islamic-economy-2013.pdf.

Reuters, T. (2013b). Islamic interbank benchmark rate. Retrieved March 11, 2013, from http://thomsonreuters.com/products_services/financial/islamic_interbank_benchmark_rate/.

Rigobon, R., & Sack, B. (2003). Measuring the reaction of monetary policy to the stock market. *Quarterly Journal of Economics*, *118*(2), 639–669.

Usmani, M.T. (2002). *An Introduction to Islamic Finance*. Hague, Netherlands: Kluwer Law International.

Chapter 11

Islamic versus conventional equities

'Understanding the law without appreciating its sociological, psychological, and moral significance is like knowing the recipe of a dessert without appreciating the delicacies of the flavors. The grandeur of law should be appreciated under the light of the magnanimity of the other influences. The poignancy of the law could never do justice to the gravity of the crime. The law might define it as soliciting a favor from someone through the use of force. It is when the imagination manifests the torture and the horrors to life, when the brutality experienced by the body and the soul heightens in valor, does the act achieve its reality and become an abomination. To be deplored, despised, shunned, and prohibited. The understanding of the act is elucidated when God's anger and the societal rage is aligned. Then the prohibition of God provides a further motivation for the believer not to indulge in the crime and the sin. The resonance between the societal and the religious consciousness is in perfect harmony. The purpose of the law is to clarify the magnitude of the punishment, to settle the dispute, and to establish the abomination of the act such that the immorality of the action is not questioned even by the criminal'.

The repulsion of the debt contract is hidden to people who benefit from it during periods of gain. Its unacceptability is only obvious to the poor, who are penalized with higher rates, culminating in the continuous fear of not being able to repay. To the rich and the ambitious, the problem is manifested during financial crisis, like the one we experienced in 2008. Periods of massive default see the plight of the rich become similar to that of the poor who remain in a state of perpetual default. The success of debt and an economy based on that would remain as long as there is growth, when the lender and the borrower are both happy. The debt fuels growth and the growth fuels more debt. Only when the world is in a recession does the realization emerge that the emperor is wearing no clothes. Until that shout, people remain in a state of glory, fascinated by the idea of the emperor's nakedness.

A clichéd analogy to explain Islamic finance is that of the institution of marriage. How the religious proclamations, the offer, and the acceptance in the presence of witnesses makes sacrilegious the act of marriage, and the absence of which makes it forbidden. There are clearly more similarities between marriage and a debt contract. During moments of success and strength, its value cannot be completely appreciated. During the upturn, the downturn seems elusive. It is during difficult times that the value it offers is manifested. Many people's belief in the institution of marriage is rekindled in old age. They would talk about the magnanimity of the relationship with their last few struggling breaths. The same may be true for the prohibition of Riba.

11.1 Introduction

In Chapter 4, the robustness of the Islamic banking system, relative to its conventional counterpart, was discussed in the light of the global financial crisis of 2008. Many studies have shown that during economically turbulent times, Islamic banks have performed better globally, have shown greater stability, and have remained fairly insulated from financial shocks.[1] It is argued that the risk-sharing foundation of the industry actually results in a lower overall macroeconomic risk in the banking industry, impeding the formation of asset price bubbles (which ultimately result in a financial crisis). The chapter highlighted the central role of the conventional banking industry and *risk-shifting* debt contracts in the creation of the global crisis. Interest-bearing debt is widely blamed for the 2008 global recession. In the aftermath of the crisis, the performance of Islamic *risk-sharing* structures came under greater scrutiny as a potentially safer alternative to the conventional model. This stream of research was extended to Islamic equities to understand whether their unique characteristics, particularly low debt, enabled them to outperform conventional equities and in turn act as a hedge or shelter for investors during periods of turmoil. In this chapter, we examine both the theoretical argument and data implications emerging from the comparison of conventional and Islamic equities to determine the existence of any consistent relationship. Specifically, we address the question of whether Islamic stock can act as a hedge during relatively calm periods and a shelter in times of systematic economic and financial crisis.[2]

11.2 The structure of Islamic equities

The term *Islamic equity* or *Islamic stock* refers to the stocks and shares of a restricted group of entities which are carefully screened against a certain criterion enabling them to comply with Islamic law. In order to qualify as an Islamic equity, there are a number of financial filters which are applied during the screening process. These filters are designed to exclude firms engaged in activities prohibited under Shariah. For example, the Dow Jones Islamic Market Index applies two levels of filters. The first relates to *Industry Screens*,[3] which excludes stocks of firms from certain industries. Some of the common industry exclusions are alcohol and pork-related products, non halal meat products, conventional financial services, indecent entertainment, gambling, tobacco, weapons, and ammunition. Once companies have cleared this screen, the next stage of filter is that of *Financial Ratio Screens*.[4] In this step, the focus is to eliminate companies that rely heavily on non Shariah compliant debt. Entities which are heavily cash driven with low investment in physical assets will also be excluded. There are prescribed limits which the firms need to adhere to. For example, the debt to market capitalization[5] should be less than 33%. Similarly, the sum of a company's cash and interest-bearing securities divided by market capitalization and the accounts receivable divided by market capitalization must also be below 33%. Islamic equities are therefore likely to be entities with low leverage from certain (restricted) industries (excluding financial services). In a way, companies that are less financially sound and are more prone to financial distress are excluded from the list.

The investor base of Islamic equities is also distinct in being dominated by Shariah conscious investors, who may derive utility from an investment's adherence to Islamic principles rather than focusing exclusively on the risk and return features of the equity.

11.3 Diversification benefits

During periods of economic crisis, investors are keen to diversify their portfolio into relatively safer options to provide a safe haven from extreme conditions. Traditionally, when conventional equity markets become turbulent, commodities such as gold have been considered a safer alternative by investors. This phenomenon was observed during the 2008 global crisis when an impressive performance was observed in the gold market in contrast with other types of assets. However, an unexplored area is whether diversification within the same asset class, i.e., conventional and Islamic equities, can be beneficial. Can Islamic equities also provide diversification benefits for investors during a crisis? In particular, do they possess *hedge* and/or *haven* properties? The term *hedge* has been used in the literature[6] to describe the lack of correlation or negative correlation of an Islamic stock with a conventional stock. This does not necessarily mean that it will reduce losses during crisis periods since the possibility of contagion still exists. *Haven*, however, specifically refers to property that provides a shelter or favorable opportunity to the investor in crisis conditions. Stocks possessing strong *haven* characteristics will be negatively correlated with conventional stocks during such extreme periods. Figure 11.1 provides some insights into this question of diversification and shows the movements of the Dow Jones Islamic stock price index and the gold price index during the period from August 1 to December 31, 2007. There is visibly a strong co-movement of both asset classes, which suggests that Islamic stock could also provide a strong haven during turmoil periods.

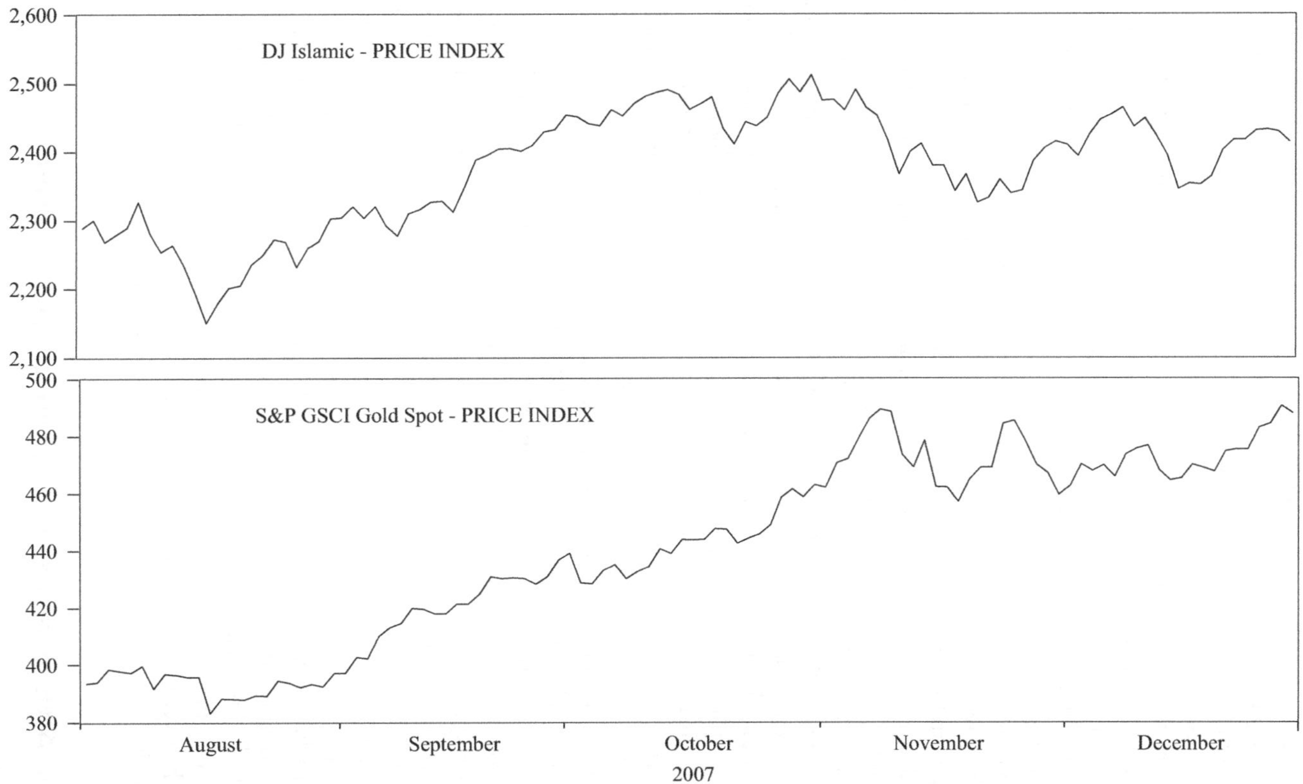

Figure 11.1 Dow Jones Islamic Price Index vs S&P GSCI Gold Spot Price Index (Graph from Azad et al., 2018, 4)

11.4 The performance of Islamic equities

In the period following the 2008 crisis, a significant body of research suggested that Islamic equities outperform conventional counterparts in periods of recession.[7] Some studies have extended this argument further to claim that Islamic equity indices perform better than their conventional equivalents in non-crisis periods as well.[8] Different reasons have been put forward for this superior performance. For example, the distinct features of Islamic finance, namely freedom from interest, uncertainty, and ambiguity,[9] are seen as some of the key distinguishing factors which enable Islamic finance products to outperform their conventional counterparts.

Another line of argument concerns the underlying structure of Islamic equities. As discussed earlier, a primary characteristic of Islamic equities is that they comprise firms with low leverage. *Prima facie*, the assertion that firms with low debt may have an advantage is somewhat counter intuitive in light of traditional capital structure theories. The pecking order model suggests that when firms need to raise capital, they may prefer to utilize internal funds before seeking external sources of funding. When external funding is required, the preference may be for debt over equity. The presence of asymmetric information between the managers and shareholders means that the issuance of equity sends a signal to the market of over-valuation of the company's shares and hence pushes the share price down. This in turn suggests that higher debt results in a greater value of the firm.[10] Another traditional perspective toward debt and its impact on firm value comes from the trade-off theory. This suggests that there are pros and cons to having debt in a firm's capital structure. As long as the benefits (the tax shield of interest) outweigh the negatives (the financial distress costs), firms will prefer to issue debt and this will enhance the value of the firm. The marginal benefit is greatest at lower levels of debt. Firms therefore manage this trade-off in order to decide on their optimal levels of debt.

In contrast to traditional theories, a relatively more recent perspective is that the benefit of debt is dominant during periods of growth and economic prosperity. At such times, the risk of default is low and the potential returns from investments are high. Firms will therefore favor debt and this will positively impact their value. However, periods of economic downturn give rise to the externality of debt. At such times, the default risk, which imposes an additional cost on both firms and banks, increases and hence debt contracts become less optimal. This suggests that during periods of economic downturn and crisis, stocks of firms with lower levels of debt would perform better than those of highly levered entities. As a result, Islamic stocks, which have lower debt levels by design, may outperform conventional stock in periods of turmoil.

11.5 A theoretical and empirical perspective

Through the development of a mathematical model, Azad, Azmat, Chazi, and Ahsan (2018) show how Islamic stocks might provide a shelter in periods of financial turbulence. There are three underlying assumptions. Firstly, Islamic stocks have lower levels of debt and are therefore expected to perform better than high-debt equities during periods of crisis (in line with the arguments given earlier). Secondly, Islamic stock markets are less efficient and less responsive to the effects of a downturn since they operate in a relatively smaller universe with less choices available for the Shariah conscious investor. The third assumption is that Shariah conscious investors would generate greater utility from the *Islamic* classification of the instruments as opposed to just risk and return (thus providing a greater source of rigidity in a downturn).

The theoretical model was further supported by collecting and testing conventional stock market indices of differing frequencies (daily, weekly, and monthly) from developed and emerging economies for the period from January 2000 through December 2015. The data comprised a sample size of 4,166 observations for daily data, 886 observations for weekly data, and 192 observations for monthly data, and were divided into three periods. The pre-crisis period began from January 2000 through June 2007. The crisis (global financial crisis) period ranged from July 2007 to June 2008. Finally, the post-crisis period began from July 2008 through December 2015. The conventional equity data were compared with the Dow Jones Islamic Index for all three periods, and the results were analyzed using quantile regression techniques to determine whether any pattern of hedge or haven could be established for Islamic equities *vis-à-vis* the conventional indices in the pre-crisis, crisis, and post-crisis periods.[11]

The data suggested that from the period January 2007 through December 2008 for all economies under study there was a clear drop in correlation during the peak of the global crisis. For some markets, the correlations showed a steep drop (such as Greece, MSCI Euro, MSCI Emerging, the UK, Hong Kong, Japan), while for others they showed considerable volatility during the crisis (such as Australia, France, MSCI Asia Pacific, India, and Switzerland).

The results for the daily frequency suggest some (limited) hedging in the pre-crisis period. However, the crisis and post-crisis data show that Islamic equities act as a hedge and haven for most markets. The results from the weekly data suggest that in the crisis and post-crisis periods, Islamic equities act as a haven for most of the markets, and, similarly, the monthly data also provide strong evidence of the hedge and haven properties of Islamic stocks in most markets for all periods under study. Collectively, the results suggest that Islamic equities could be considered by short-term and long-term investors looking to diversify their portfolio and minimize risk and losses in normal as well as crisis periods.

11.6 Concluding remarks

The chapter compares the performance of Islamic equities with conventional equities for pre-crisis, crisis, and post-crisis periods. Literature generally supports the assertion that Islamic equities are stronger performers during periods of crisis. This is attributed primarily to the lower levels of debt, lower liquidity of Islamic markets, and the religious consciousness of the investor base. This argument is strengthened with empirical data for the period from 2000 through 2015 showing that Islamic equities will act as a hedge overall and provide a safe haven from crisis for most conventional global equities. The findings are of particular relevance to portfolio managers and investors since they strongly suggest that Islamic equities do indeed hold diversification benefits in periods of economic turmoil. In order to ensure the sustainability of this position, it is important that the Shariah compliance aspect not be compromised. This will ensure the continued trust and confidence of investors and portfolio managers and will allow Islamic equities to maintain this advantage over conventional securities.

Notes

1 For further details, refer to Askari (2012) and Beck et al. (2013).
2 The inspiration for the chapter comes from the paper by Azad et al. (2018).
3 www.investment-and-finance.net/islamic-finance/i/industry-screens.html, retrieved March 18, 2018.
4 www.investment-and-finance.net/islamic-finance/f/financial-ratio-screens.html, retrieved March 18, 2018.
5 'Market capitalization' is defined as the '24-month trailing average market capitalization'.
6 The terms *hedge* and *haven* used in the chapter have been taken from Baur and Lucey (2010).
7 For further details, refer to Al-Khazali et al. (2014), Hoepner et al. (2011), Rubio et al. (2012), and Ho et al. (2014).
8 For further details, refer to Charles et al. (2015).
9 For further details, refer to Dewi et al. (2010).
10 For further details, refer to Myers and Majluf (1984).
11 Further details of the methodology and models used can be obtained from Azad et al. (2018). The chapter only provides a summary of the key findings.

Bibliography

Ajmi, A., Hammoudeh, S., Nguyen, D., & Sarafrazi, S. (2014). How strong are the causal relationships between Islamic stock market and conventional financial systems? Evidence from linear and nonlinear tests. *Journal of International Financial Markets, Institutions & Money, 28*, 213–227.

Al-Khazali, O., Lean, H., & Samet, A. (2014). Do Islamic stock indexes outperform conventional stock indexes? A stochastic dominance approach. *Pacific-Basin Finance Journal, 28*, 29–46.

Ashraf, D., & Mohammad, N. (2014). Matching perception with the reality: Performance of Islamic equity investments. *Pacific-Basin Finance Journal, 28*, 175–189.

Askari, H. (2012). Islamic finance, risk sharing, and international financial stability. *Yale Journal of International Affairs*. Retrieved September 10, 2018 from http://yalejournal.org/article_post/islamic-finance-risk-sharing-and-international-financial-stability/.

Ayub, M. (2009). *Understanding Islamic Finance*. Chichester, UK: John Wiley & Sons.
Azad, A.S.M.S., Azmat, S., Chazi, A., & Ahsan, A. (2018). Sailing with the non-conventional stocks when there is no place to hide. *Journal of International Financial Markets Institutions and Money*. (In press). doi: 10.1016/j.intfin.2018.04.001.
Baur, D.G., & Lucey, B.M. (2010). Is gold a hedge or a safe haven? An analysis of stocks, bonds and gold. *The Financial Review, 45*, 217–229.
Baur, D.G., & McDermott, T.K. (2010). Is gold a safe haven? International evidence. *Journal of Banking and Finance, 34*, 1886–1898.
Beck, T., Demirgüç-Kunt, A., & Merrouche, O. (2013). Islamic vs. conventional banking: Business model, efficiency and stability. *Journal of Banking and Finance, 37*, 433–447.
Cappiello, L., Engle, R., & Sheppard, K. (2006). Asymmetric dynamics in the correlations of global equity and bond returns. *Journal of Financial Econometrics, 4*, 537–572.
Chapra, U. (2008). The global financial crisis: Can Islamic finance help minimize the severity and frequency of such a crisis in the future? Lecture delivered at the inaugural session of the Eighth Harvard University Forum on Islamic Finance held on 19–20 April, 2008.
Charles, A., Darné, O., & Pop, A. (2015). Risk and ethical investment: Empirical evidence from Dow Jones Islamic indexes. *Research in International Business and Finance, 35*, 33–56.
Dewandaru, G., Rizvi, S.A.R., Masih, R., Masih, M., & Alhabshi, S.O. (2014). Stock market co-movements: Islamic versus conventional equity indices with multi-time-scales analysis. *Economic Systems, 38*, 553–571.
Dewi, M. K., Sulaiman, M., & Ferdian, I. R. (2010). Efficiency of Islamic banks in selected member countries of the Organisation of Islamic Conference. *International Journal of Monetary Economics and Finance, 3*(2), 177–205.
Ebrahim, M.S., Jaafar, A., Omar, F.A., & Salleh, M.O. (2016). Can Islamic injunctions indemnify the structural flaws of securitized debt? *Journal of Corporate Finance, 37*, 271–286.
El Alaoui, A.O., Bacha, O.I., Masih, M., & Asutay, M. (2016). Shari'ah screening, market risk and contagion: A multi-country analysis. *Journal of Economic Behavior & Organization, 132*, 93–112.
El Qorchi, M. (2005). *Islamic Finance Gears Up. Finance and Development*. Washington, DC: International Monetary Fund.
Fama, E.F., & French, K.R. (2002). Testing trade-off and pecking order predictions about dividends and debt. *Review of Financial Studies, 15*, 1–33.
Farooq, M., & Zaheer, S. (2015). Are Islamic banks more resilient during financial panics? *Pacific Economic Review, 20*, 101–124.
Hammoudeh, S., Mensi, W., Reboredo, J., & Nguyen, D. (2014). Dynamic dependence of the global Islamic equity index with global conventional equity market indices and risk factors. *Pacific-Basin Finance Journal, 30*, 189–206.
Hasan, M., & Dridi, J. (2010). *The Effects of the Global Crisis on Islamic and Conventional Banks: A Comparative Study*. IMF Working Paper 10/201. Washington, DC: International Monetary Fund.
Ho, C.S.F., Rahman, N.A.A., Yusuf, N.H.M., & Zamzamin, Z. (2014). Performance of global Islamic versus conventional share Indices: International evidence. *Pacific-Basin Finance Journal, 28*, 110–121.

Hoepner, A.G., Rammal, H.G., & Rezec, M. (2011). Islamic mutual funds' financial performance and international investment style: Evidence from 20 countries. *The European Journal of Finance, 17*, 829–850.

Hussein, K., & Omran, M. (2005). Ethical investment revisited: Evidence from Dow Jones Islamic indexes. *Journal of Investing, 14*, 105–124.

International Monetary Fund (IMF). (2015). *World Economic and Financial Surveys, Regional Economic Outlook, Middle East and Central Asia*. Washington, DC: IMF, 91–96.

Majdoub, J., & Mansour, W. (2014). Islamic equity market integration and volatility spillover between emerging and US stock markets. *North American Journal of Economics and Finance, 29*, 452–470.

Mian, A., & Sufi, A. (2010). The great recession: Lessons from microeconomic data. *The American Economic Review, 100*, 51–56.

Mian, A., & Sufi, A. (2011). House prices, home equity-based borrowing, and the US household leverage crisis. *The American Economic Review, 101*, 2132–2156.

Mian, A., & Sufi, A. (2015). *House of Debt: How They (And You) Caused the Great Recession, and How We Can Prevent It from Happening Again*. Chicago, IL: University of Chicago Press.

Myers, S.C., & Majluf, N.S. (1984). Corporate financing and investment decisions when firms have information that investors do not have. *Journal of Financial Economics, 13*, 187–221.

Narayan, P.K., & Phan, D.H.B. (2016). Momentum strategies for Islamic stocks. *Pacific-Basin Finance Journal 40*, 211–223.

Naughton, S., & Naughton, T. (2000). Religion, ethics and stock trading: The case of an Islamic equities market. *Journal of Business Ethics, 23*, 145–159.

Obaidullah, M. (2001). Ethics and efficiency in Islamic stock markets. *International Journal of Islamic Financial Services, 3*, 1–10.

Rubio, J.F., Hasan, M.K., & Hesham, J.M. (2012). Non-parametric performance measurement of international and Islamic mutual funds. *Accounting Research Journal, 25*, 208–226.

Song, M.I., & Oosthuizen, C. (2014). *Islamic Banking Regulation and Supervision: Survey Results and Challenges (No. 14-220)*. Washington, DC: IMF.

Walkshausl, C., & Lobe, S. (2012). Islamic investing. *Review of Financial Economics, 21*, 53–62.

Yilmaz, M., Sensoy, A., Ozturk, K., & Hacihasanoglu, E. (2015). Cross-sectoral interactions in Islamic equity markets. *Pacific-Basin Finance Journal, 32*, 1–20.

Chapter 12

Charity in Islamic banks

A distinguishing feature?

I was sitting with an old friend, an entrepreneur who had had experienced success like few others I had known. A self-made billionaire oozing with excitement and exuberance. The topic of our conversation was the horrific incident that had shocked the country, the death of 150 people, including young children and women, the casualty of an oil tanker blast. Considered to be one of the worst accidents of fire explosion in the world, an oil tanker of a big multinational oil company had toppled over in the middle of a road, gushing oil everywhere—a situation that should have called for rapid containment. The catastrophic scene became an unfortunate opportunity for the poor living in nearby villages. Faced with energy shortages and rising oil prices, the villagers living around the area saw it as a blessing in disguise, a gift brought about by nature, a moment of wealth redistribution. The poor came in large numbers to collect the free oil, risking their lives when they should have been running away from it. Families sent their young ones to fetch oil using their household utensils. It became a competition for who could collect the most. Motorcyclists were stopping to fill their tanks, thinking that Eid had arrived a few days early. A sudden unexpected moment saw their smiles vanish and turn to horror. Momentary happiness turned into perpetual grief as the tanker exploded, killing indiscriminately all those standing around with their false hopes. It marked the end of life for many. For their loved ones, who would experience the traumatic event for days and months, it was the end of life as they knew it. My friend, the self-made billionaire, blamed the greed of the poor who had risked it all for an inconsequential amount. He criticized their irrationality and stupidity, an outcome of their materialistic nature. For him, the villagers were a symbol of what society should shun. I sat there listening to him, thinking about the simplicity with which he was taking things for granted, things that many had died for. Ignoring the abject poverty which may have caused the villagers to show an utter disregard for what was most precious for what was least. How many days of hunger could cause someone to do such a thing? How many times would they have to look at others with envy and desire for these petty possessions? In that moment, I realized that the law made by the privileged can never cater for those who lack it.

12.1 Introduction

A recurrent criticism of Islamic banks is that they have not lived up to the expectations in fulfilling the greater objectives of Islamic economics, particularly creating equitable distribution of wealth in society. Profit maximization is the ultimate goal of conventional banks with very little (or no) attention devoted toward ethical considerations such as fairness, equity, or exploitation of the weak.[1] The key motivating factor behind the prohibition of Riba in Islamic finance *is* to eliminate exploitation and injustice. This is considered to be a necessary objective of the Islamic economic system which has at its core the goals of socioeconomic justice and fairness for all. One of the means to achieve this is by forbidding the charging of interest on the borrowing and lending of funds, which, one would assume, should automatically result in a fairer and more equitable society. In this chapter, we focus on a unique aspect of Islamic banking where the banks replace the charging of the forbidden interest with a mandatory penalty. The primary difference between the two forms of excess charge is that for the conventional bank, interest contributes to their profit, while for the Islamic bank, the excess is given out in charity. In this way, it is a contribution toward societal welfare. In this chapter, we understand the dynamics of this charity as given by Islamic banks.

12.2 Penalty versus charity

As already defined, Riba is any predetermined excess over and above the principal amount in a loan contract. Islamic banks circumvent this prohibition by involving a real asset, so the loan contract converts into a trade contract. In the process, a debt is created which is paid periodically by the customer to the bank. The excess that Islamic banks charge is imbedded in the price of the asset; it has to be decided *ex-ante*. Once the contract is signed and the ownership of the asset transfers, the banks cannot charge any further excess to the customer, even if payment is delayed. This would be considered equivalent to the forbidden Riba. This feature of an Islamic financial product makes it highly impractical. In the absence of any disincentive to return the money, which is the case in a traditional loan contract, the investors are unlikely to return the money on time. The earlier scholars of Islamic finance pondered over this problem and came up with an ingenious alternative. They allowed Islamic banks to charge a penalty on delayed payment, with the added condition that the money would be given in charity. The fact that money is not kept by the Islamic banks or becomes a part of its profitability means that it does not violate the traditional definition of Riba where the lender benefits from the borrower with the delay in payment. Here, the cost is imposed on the borrower, but it does not benefit the lender. The nature of the charity contract is such that the lender has little to gain from it, which is in sharp contrast to a conventional contract, where the lender benefits from the delay and in some cases (especially in the case of credit cards) wants the customer to prolong the returning of the principal.

On the consumer's side too there can be the issue of the failure to return the money in time. However, in this case, charity represents the cost of Shariah compliance. If Islamic banks end up making a deal which is non Shariah compliant, the amount has to be given in charity. Charity is therefore a deterrent against the problems of 'moral hazard'. Moral hazard occurs when the party with more information about its actions or intentions (the bank) has a tendency or incentive to behave inappropriately (or take more risks) from the perspective of the party with less information (the consumer). Charity will act to prevent the banks from deviating from Shariah compliance. In an emerging and relatively nascent industry, such costs of noncompliance are to be expected until such a time as the industry matures to absolute perfection. In the meantime, Islamic banks and windows can cleanse such doubtful capital by contributing this portion of their profit toward charity. The nature of charity is a distinguishing feature of Islamic finance, emerging purely out of the need for practicality and not linked with the pursuit of profit. This aspect is in sharp contrast to its conventional counterparts where the beneficiary from noncompliance (on the part of the consumer) is the bank itself.

Understanding the patterns of charity giving and spending provides valuable insights into the cost of Islamic financing. It is also an aspect that supports the greater vision of Islamic finance, which is to contribute to society, and hence is a direct response to those critical of the field on the grounds that it fails to contribute to social justice, equity, and fairness in society. Charity also provides a means to boost the industry and the country's economy. For example, if the charity is spent on education, it raises the country's human capital, which in turn boosts the economy in the long run.

In this chapter, various questions are explored on the charity payouts of banks. For example, how significant is the cost of noncompliance that Islamic banks bear, and what are the nature of the amounts they give to charity each year? What is the social impact of charity? How are Islamic banks spending such funds, and what kind of welfare projects are they supporting? We analyze empirical data from Islamic banks and Islamic windows in Pakistan from 2012 to 2014. The sample size consisted of a total of 15 banks that reported their annual charity data.

12.3 The size of the charity pie

The data suggest that the Islamic finance industry in Pakistan transferred Rs 750 million to charity. A bigger chunk of this amount was contributed by the five big fully fledged Islamic banks; they transferred Rs 404 million (54% of the total to charity). The ten Islamic windows contributed Rs 346 million (46%). On average, Islamic banks transferred Rs 27 million per bank each year, and Islamic windows Rs 12 million per window each year.

For a country like Pakistan, where non-profit and charity organizations rely heavily on support from private organizations, the charity from Islamic banks may offer a useful contribution to some welfare projects. A particular challenge facing these organizations, when relying on charity from Islamic banks, may be the volatility of these contributions. In certain years they may be high, owing to a larger number of defaults or mistakes made by Islamic banks. In other years they may be low. Our data suggested that the highest amount collected in a particular year for an Islamic bank was around Rs 83 million, while the lowest amount was Rs 9 million. For the Islamic window, the lowest amount was zero. This volatility in the amount of charity collected may increase the risk faced by organizations relying on charity from Islamic banks. It may also mean that it would be difficult to envisage long-term projects using this money. In many cases, the charity, as and when it becomes available, should help address the short-term needs of these social organizations. Another interesting pattern that we observed in the data was that there appeared to be a decline in the charity amount over the years. Over the three-year period, the percentage decline in the charity amount was 12% for the entire industry, 17.43% for the Islamic banks, and 6% for the Islamic windows. Since the data sample was too small to make any meaningful generalization, we collected anecdotal evidence to corroborate these findings. We found that in the initial years after the inception of Islamic banking, the charity amount collected was much greater than in the later years. This was due to the fact that many of the Islamic banks were making many more financial mistakes related to considerations of Shariah compliance, and so the money had to be given out in charity. As they became more efficient over the years, they made fewer mistakes, which resulted in lower contributions to charity. In light of this, the average given to charity should decrease further in the future.

12.4 Charity contribution versus asset size

Using our data, we compared the charity contributions of Islamic banks against their asset sizes. This helped us to identify the significance of the charity contributed with respect to the size of the Islamic banking industry. It shed light on the importance of charity giving for Islamic banks—whether the act of giving is an integral part of the industry, or a goal to be maximized to comply with the higher objectives of Islamic economics, or a necessary cost of doing business for the bank to remain Shariah compliant, or something actually to be minimized.

As expected, we found that Islamic banks tend to be much larger than Islamic windows. There is also a significant variation in the asset base of different Islamic banks and windows, with the biggest Islamic bank capturing a significant part of the market share (see Figure 12.1).

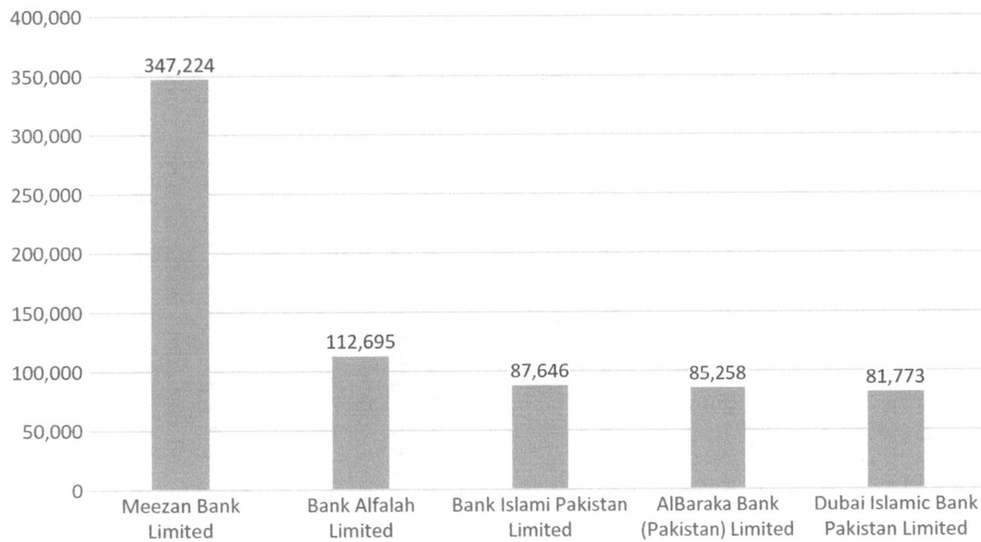

Figure 12.1 Five banks (or windows) with largest Islamic asset base size, in descending order (of their means)

In the period under review, fully fledged Islamic banks had an average asset base of approximately double that of Islamic windows (Rs 649,790 million versus Rs 352,718 million). Charity to asset base ratio for Islamic banks was 0.021%; for Islamic windows it stood at 0.033%; and for the Islamic finance banking industry it averaged 0.025% (see Table 12.1).

Even a cursory look at these numbers speaks volumes about the relevance of charity for Islamic banks. Comparing the charity amount to the total asset base, it seems obvious that giving is not an important objective—neither of the Islamic bank, nor the shareholders, nor the depositors whose money the bank manages. The charity amount seems to be a cost which the management committee of the Islamic bank is minimizing to serve the best interests of the shareholders and the depositors. The numbers may be insignificant when compared to the total asset base, but in terms of affecting the bank's profitability, it can have a slightly more significant impact. On average, the charity amount affects banks' profitability by around 1–2%.

12.5 Social distribution of charity

The data suggest that charity distribution was heavily skewed toward health, education, and social welfare respectively. Health took the lion's share (42.8%), followed by education (35.7%), and social welfare (16.5%) (see Table 12.2).

Charity spending breakdown was not publicly available for five of the ten Islamic windows (Habib Bank Limited, Habib Metropolitan Bank Limited, Soneri Bank Limited, Standard Chartered Bank (Pakistan) Limited, and United Bank Limited). For Bank Islami (Islamic Bank), the spending breakdown for 2012 was available; however, the breakdown for 2013 and 2014 was not disclosed. Charity amounts disbursed to individuals was categorized into the 'social welfare' spending stream.

The distribution of charity seems to be more an outcome of preferences of Islamic bankers and the civil society at large, rather than being driven by some higher ideals of Islamic economics. In a country like Pakistan,

Table 12.1 Charity to asset size

	Number of banks or windows	*Asset base size mean (Islamic)*	*Charity to Islamic asset base ratio (C/A, %)*
Islamic banks	05	646,790	0.021%
Islamic windows	10	352,718	0.033%
Total industry	15	999,508	0.025%

Table 12.2 Weighted average and standard deviation of percentage charity allocation (spending) by sector

	Weighted average			*Standard deviation*		
	Islamic banks	*Islamic windows*	*Total industry*	*Islamic banks*	*Islamic windows*	*Total industry*
Education	42%	21%	35.66%	25%	15%	21%
Health	42%	45%	42.80%	23%	20%	22%
Islamic microfinance	1%	0%	0.67%	5%	0%	4%
Environmental	0%	0%	0.06%	0%	0%	0%
Relief and disaster recovery	3%	7%	4.28%	5%	29%	21%
Social welfare	12%	26%	16.53%	17%	16%	18%

where education and health care are expensive and scarce, it is natural that Islamic banks have preferred to allocate a significant portion to it. It would be useful if Islamic banks could create an overarching framework where the charity amount is spent to serve some ideals of Islamic economics in a more coherent manner; this may distinguish Islamic banks from their conventional counterparts.

12.6 Concluding remarks

In this chapter, we focused on an aspect of Islamic banking which has generated quite a lot of attention from those who are critical of this practice and others who advocate its beneficial purpose for society. The ones who criticize this practice consider it as Riba in disguise, since Islamic banks charge for the delayed payment. The proponents, however, claim that the charity giving distinguishes Islamic banks from their conventional counterparts as the money is eventually spent on societal welfare. We analyzed data from Islamic banks in Pakistan to understand the dynamics of charity giving.

We found that charity giving is a practice unique to Islamic banks. For conventional banks, any excess on delayed payment is kept as a profit, providing a compensation to the conventional bank and in some cases incentivizing the bank to lend money in such a manner that the payment is delayed. For the Islamic bank, the payment charged on the excess is not an incentive as the money is given out in charity. We found that Islamic banks were involved in some worthy projects, particularly those related to providing free education and healthcare for society, which were sponsored through the allocation set aside as charity. The welfare aspect of charity giving and its role, not as a mechanism to increase bank profitability, but rather as a vehicle for promoting social welfare, make it a unique transaction unlike anything we have seen in the conventional banking sector. We also found, however, that the absence of the profit motive meant that the Islamic banks consider it a cost that is to be reduced. In a way, it seems that rather than considering it as a means to fulfill the greater purpose of Islamic economics, the banks view it as a necessary burden, a tax impeding their pursuit of profit. We found that over the years there has been a considerable decrease in the charity amount as part of a deliberate effort to minimize its cost and endure it simply for reasons of Shariah compliance rather than pursuing it as an objective for the greater good.

We also found that the impact of charity giving remains rather insignificant when pursuing the purpose of societal welfare. In a country like Pakistan with a budget of more than Rs 2 trillion, a contribution of less than Rs 1 billion by the Islamic banking industry as charity may not affect society as a whole in any meaningful way. The overall small size of charity by Islamic banks is no way proportional to the size of the Islamic finance industry as a whole. We found that while the asset base for Islamic banks had experienced a significant increase over the years, the charity pool had shrunk. For the sample under consideration, charity as a proportion of total assets for the Islamic banking industry stood at a meager 0.025%. The growth objective of the industry was visible, crowding out the pro-social giving behavior of Islamic banks. Since the charity component is a random component emerging out of the mistakes made by Islamic banks or the defaulting customers, it would be difficult for charity organizations to rely on them as a permanent source of income. This would hinder the initiation of social projects with a long-term purview. The spikes in charity funds would favor projects of a short-term nature, hence limiting its impact.

When it comes to charity giving as a distinguishing aspect of Islamic banks, there seems to be something to celebrate, as anything that deviates from the incentive to maximize profits and accumulate wealth, especially in a banking setting, is to be welcomed. Like many other aspects of Islamic banking, the component which is synchronized with the higher ideals of Islamic economics imposes a cost on Islamic banks, which eventually causes it to be somewhat marginalized. Charity giving by Islamic banks may be suffering from a similar fate.

Note

1 Ayub, M. (2007). *Understanding Islamic Finance.* London: Wiley..

Chapter 13

Rethinking Islamic finance

The limits of our understanding

Sometime ago, an old student of mine visited me. He had taken an undergraduate course on Islamic finance with me. I particularly liked him as he would always ask thought provoking questions. It was a delight to see him. He was working for a big bank in the US. I could see a twitch of guilt in him when he mentioned his occupation, for he knew about my views on conventional banking. Not wanting to be judged, he broached the subject of the prohibition of Riba. He was trying to justify that modern day banking might not be characterized as Riba. His arguments were smart, but he had heard of my counter arguments time and again. The hesitation in his voice was an indication that his conviction was weak regarding the veracity of his claims. Just to be polite, I continued the conversation, offering him rebuttals. But deep down I knew fairly well that I would never be able to convince him. For it was not the rigor of the argument and the obviousness of the truth but the pain of acceptance that was the hurdle. For believing the truth meant either living a life of guilt or bearing the pain of quitting the job, neither of which he seemed prepared for. Both these options seemed less desirable to the alternative of not accepting the obvious. Reason was clouded by desires while judgment was subjected to passion. In that moment, I felt that rationality is over rated—the higher consciousness is enslaved to the lower passions. In the guise of reason, the lower self was subjecting God to its judgment.

'What I do not desire, I do not understand and what I do not understand cannot be from God'.

The saints and the scholars of the past had realized the subtlety of this deception. They never subjected revelation to reason. Reason was always used to appreciate divine wisdom and not to judge it. As our conversation ended, the student eventually said:

'I believe in divine wisdom and I believe the orders and commandments of God abound with divine grace'.

I thought that he had come full circle. The greatest strength of the Islamic finance industry is that it is anchored in revelation, where abiding by the law is primary while the ensuing consequences are always secondary. In a way the industry remains conflicted and will remain so until the process is aligned with the outcome.

13.1 Introduction

This book explores the impact of institutions, markets, regulations, and individuals, and their interaction on the development of Islamic finance. One of the most important challenges in the Islamic finance industry is the struggle faced by the participants in understanding some of the key features of Islamic financial products and processes. Apparently, there seems to be a disconnect between the principles advocated by the scholars of Islamic economics and the products offered by the discipline. In this chapter, we offer some survey data to first understand what Islamic banking customers consider to be the main pillars of Islamic economics. Then we analyze to what extent this understanding of the field is at odds with what is practiced and preached. In this chapter, we explore some of the common arguments given against Islamic banking by those who are either critical or skeptical of the subject.

13.2 Pillars of Islamic economics

Most of the participants in our survey agreed that Islamic banking and finance is governed by the broader principles and objectives underlying the Islamic economic system. Islamic economics, in accordance with the teachings of the Quran and Sunnah, allows for the pursuit of wealth while placing an ethical bound on the actions of individuals and institutions to ensure that they act in the best interests of society. As a result, it represents a more balanced approach as opposed to other economic systems, i.e., capitalism and socialism. While capitalism considers pure profit motivation without any regard to society as completely rational, socialism on the other hand does not allow any form of private property or individual wealth maximization. Conventional banking is a product of capitalism and is thus incompatible with many of the requirements of the Islamic economic system. Islamic banks are, for example, required to abstain from certain elements of the capitalist system such as Riba, Gharar, and Maisir. Most of the survey participants thought that unlike conventional banks, Islamic banks are not purely profit-driven entities and have social responsibilities as well. They are required to promote social welfare by working toward the betterment of society through pursuing goals such as the eradication of poverty. Thus, in aggregate, there seems to be a consensus that while abstaining from Riba, Gharar, and Maisir, Islamic banking should also aim toward the fulfillment of socioeconomic objectives and the creation of a just society.

The participants suggested that the objectives of the Islamic financial system should be aligned with those of the Islamic economic system, and therefore a clear understanding of the broader underlying objectives of the latter are required prior to proceeding with the finer intricacies of Islamic banking. The Islamic economic system has been defined differently by a number of scholars. The goal of Islamic economics is the promotion of justice and creation of a welfare society. Capitalism and socialism are two extreme forms of economic systems. The salient features of a capitalist system are the prevalence of free markets, ownership of private property, production for profit, and wealth accumulation. The pursuit of wealth by individuals and firms is considered to be the rational objective of all members of such economies with little or no regard for social goals or ethical aspects such as increasing poverty. Such aggressive pursuit of wealth at an individual level is said to result in economic growth and development for society at large. Capitalist systems have become associated with individualism where social welfare is considered to be an outcome of selfish pursuits. At the other end of the spectrum lies the socialist perspective toward economics, which focuses on centrally owned property and non-market motivation for production. Whereas socialism stands for alleviating the income inequality in society, capitalism necessitates distribution of income on the basis of contribution toward production, hence implying unequal distribution.

The participants thought that between these two extremes, the Islamic economic system requires its members to adopt a more balanced approach. While it enables the pursuit of wealth, the underlying condition for this pursuit is the strict adherence to principles of justice and fairness to the entire society. Just as with the free market system, an essential part of the Islamic economic philosophy is the ownership of private property and enterprise, market mechanisms, and competition; however, a fundamental feature is its reliance on distributive justice[1] and a comprehensive set of ethical principles and values to guide all decision making. The presence of these strict guidelines results in significant differences between the capitalist and Islamic approaches on conducting business. Furthermore, freely functioning markets, while permitted, need government supervision to ensure that there is no undue advantage given to the influential and stronger segments of a society. Therefore, an Islamic system is said to be free not only from the exploitation and ever increasing poverty gap that characterize capitalism but also by the class struggles and stringent restrictions associated with socialism.

The achievement of such an economic system which ensures distributive justice and equality requires certain rules or norms to be followed universally and without question. These key injunctions are divine rulings and include prohibiting any transactions involving the charging of commercial interest ('Riba'); excessive uncertainty ('Gharar' and 'Maisir'), for example gambling or speculation; the redistribution scheme of *zakat* to shorten the gap between the rich and the poor; and engagement in enterprise to earn a just return provided the risk of loss is also assumed by the investor. Apart from these procedural injunctions, principles of Islamic economics require members of the society to behave altruistically toward the needs of the less privileged. Every action and decision requires careful ethical considerations. Trade and profit are permissible only if done within the bounds of Shariah, making it binding for human beings to concomitantly focus on the societal impact of their activities.

13.3 Barriers to understanding Islamic finance

Despite its amazing growth, the phenomenon of Islamic banking has not received unanimous appreciation. Along with its increasing group of supporters who consider it a Shariah compliant alternative to conventional banking, the concept of Islamic banking also has some critics. Skeptics of contemporary Islamic banking argue that it is a mere change of jargon, and decades after its introduction, much of Islamic banking and finance is still indistinguishable from its conventional counterparts. To understand the reasons behind these different viewpoints, we conducted surveys and interviews to determine some of the major objections to Islamic banking. Also, we then put forward these arguments to proponents of Islamic finance to understand their responses to the criticisms. Interviewees comprised a mix of undergraduate students and people working in the corporate and banking sectors. A total of 50 interviews were conducted, and the responses were analyzed using a standard qualitative analysis process. The various arguments and objections given against the current practice of Islamic banking and their corresponding frequency can be seen in Figure 13.1.

The main arguments given against Islamic banking and the counter arguments offered by the interviewers are now briefly summarized.

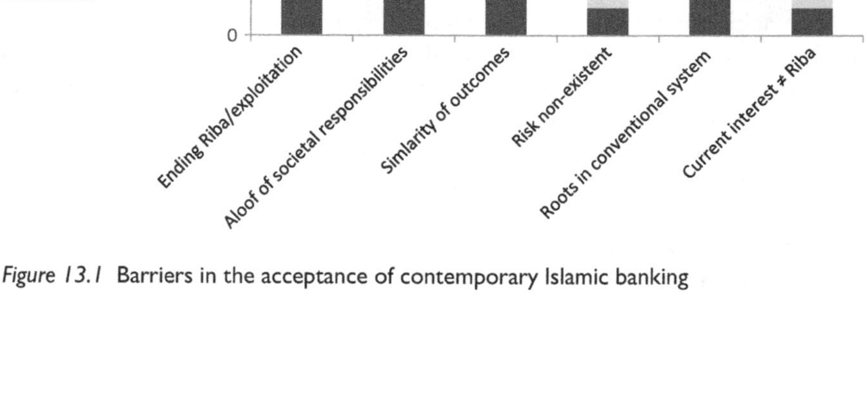

Figure 13.1 Barriers in the acceptance of contemporary Islamic banking

(i) Ending Riba/exploitation

Arguments given: The argument here is that the purpose of Islamic banking is to end exploitation, and this is the underlying reason why Riba was declared haram. According to this viewpoint, Islamic banks should only extend interest-free loans. Since today Islamic banks charge high premiums, they are equally, if not more, exploitative than their conventional counterparts. Even the charging of the late payment penalty by Islamic banks is impermissible in Islam (since this effectively falls under the definition of Riba); yet this is a common practice among Islamic banks.

Response: As far as the provision of interest-free loans is concerned, while this is encouraged by Shariah, it is not a compulsion. Rather, it is at the discretion of individuals or the State in some cases and not economic entities. Furthermore, this is not a sound proposition from an economic perspective if one considers the simple question of where the funds would come from if banks denied a return to depositors. Islam is not against the concept of profit making. The issue it stresses is how that profit is earned. Generating a return through interest-based lending is prohibited, since this leads to unequal distribution of wealth as a result of the lender not having a share in the risks or rewards of the investment and, therefore, results in exploitation. Under Islamic banking, however, the structuring of transactions is such that the lending institution bears additional risks not borne in the conventional setting, which ensures that this scheme is in fact non-exploitative, since the risk of loss is shared by the lender. Thus, the return charged by Islamic institutions is not Riba, whereas conventional banks do not bear any additional risks and charge predetermined rates of interest classifying the return made as Riba.

Regarding the objection against the imposition of penalties, this is considered necessary to deter willfull defaulters, since we live in a society that is filled with people who take undue advantage of rule relaxations. This amount is not utilized by the bank but is given to charity, and Shariah approves of this practice. Reference should also be made to the decision of the *fiqh* council[2] whereby it is stated that the penalty provision would not be binding if the client proves that the default was a consequence of circumstances beyond his control or when he proves that his breach of contract has not brought about any loss to the bank.

(ii) Non-fulfillment of social welfare role

Arguments given: While the mandated role of Islamic banks is to ensure the economic and social welfare of the community, Islamic banking today is devoid of its true spirit and has developed a completely commercial outlook. Islamic banks operate merely as profit-driven commercial enterprises and are aloof to their societal role. Like their capitalist counterparts, they offer services only to the rich and are playing an important role in making them richer while poor people are being denied this privilege. Thus they are equally contributing to the increasing gap between the rich and the poor, whereas they should have acted as agents of regulating the distribution of wealth.

Response: The commercial motives of Islamic banks are not in violation of Shariah. Shariah does not demand any members of society—including financial institutions—expend their entire surplus in charitable or welfare activities. The role of Islamic financial institutions is the mobilization and efficient allocation of resources, which is being achieved through Riba-free asset-based investments and the provision of risk capital.

(iii) Similarity of outcomes

Arguments given: Islamic banking instruments are exact replicas of conventional banking instruments. They serve the same purpose, and the final outcome in terms of rates charged in both cases is identical; for instance, Murabahah is the same as a conventional loan and Ijarah is similar to a conventional lease. Conventional terms have been given Islamic names to exploit the religious sentiments of people and to lure them to convert to Islamic banking.

Response: Islamic financial institutions are operating in a competitive environment alongside their conventional counterparts. They can, therefore, not charge rates that are significantly different from them and thus they use the same benchmark rates. The use of benchmarks makes the administration by the bank's management easy and transparent, but it does not imply similarity of procedure. The underlying procedure in the two cases is entirely different and compliant with the rules of Shariah. Conventional bank's transactions are based on money while those of Islamic banks are based on assets. Thus, where conventional banks employ benchmarks to price their money-based transactions, Islamic banks use them to price their asset-based transactions. Islamic banks do not provide loans but sell the desired commodity after bearing the risk of its ownership at a price that remains, even if a customer defaults. In Ijarah and Murabahah, they bear the risk of the assets. If the asset gets destroyed and the amount from Takaful[3] does not completely cover the loss, they cannot pass that loss onto the customer.

(iv) Islamic banks do not bear any risk

Arguments given: While Islamic banking is averse to the concept of risk-free return, it is not practiced in reality. Islamic banks, like conventional banks, bear no risk as their balance sheets show that they have never suffered a loss. In the case of Murabahah, for instance, Islamic banks only notionally assume risk because in case something happens to the commodity, the risk is always passed onto third-party insurance companies.

Response: Islamic banking is risky by its very nature, and while this inherent risk can be reduced by risk management tools, it cannot be totally evaded.

Conventional banks guarantee a risk-free return, but Islamic banks engage in business activities which can result in either a profit or a loss and hence they do take on additional risk. They concluded that provided they stay within the bounds of Shariah, Islamic banks are allowed to practice risk mitigation measures, and this does not invalidate the underlying Shariah compliance of the product.

(v) Depositors do not bear risk

Arguments given: Depositors of Islamic banks should neither be guaranteed a fixed income nor the security of their investment; however, this is true only theoretically as in normal practice the depositors do get fixed returns and Islamic banks have never passed on losses to the depositors.

Response: The reason returns are generally fixed for the depositor is because Islamic banks structure their Islamic investment products in instruments like Murabahah, which provide fixed returns. Also, the investment portfolio of Islamic banks is sufficiently diversified to minimize the chances of loss for the bank and its depositors. Furthermore, Islamic banks also create a profit reserve against which they offset future possible losses, and hence there is never a need to pass on losses to depositors.

(vi) Roots in conventional system—linkage of pricing mechanism to KIBOR and TVM

Arguments given: The contemporary Islamic banking system has its roots in the capitalist system and not in Shariah since, like conventional banks, Islamic banks use KIBOR[4] and the process of discounting to price their instruments—both approaches being products of capitalism.

Response: Firstly, Islamic banks do not make use of the time value of money in a conventional way. However, since trading and leasing are parts of their activities, they can legitimately incorporate the time factor in order to price their goods or usufructs. However, Islamic banks do not and cannot alter the receivable originally created in any circumstance. A further argument is that Islamic banks use the time value of money to price goods and products but not to price money or debt instruments.

In terms of the objection to using KIBOR, just like businesses operating in a competitive environment, Islamic banks require benchmark or reference rates to price their goods and services. Islamic banks are competing for the same sources of funds, in an industry dominated by their conventional counterparts. Thus, they are required to use KIBOR, the benchmark for the formal conventional market, to remain competitive.

(vii) Current interest rate ≠ Riba

Arguments given: The ban on Riba was placed when poor people who borrowed money for consumptive purposes were made to pay back a higher amount. This increase was purely exploitative since it would put the poor person into debt for life. Modern interest is neither a huge amount nor is it imposed on poor people, but rather huge multinationals that take loans for production and make a substantial amount of money. Since the rationale behind the prohibition of Riba no longer exists, modern interest does not come within the domain of Riba.

Response: If one considers the *Illat* (reason) and *Hikmat* (wisdom) of the prohibition of Riba, it can be seen that the *Illat* of Riba is *any predetermined increase* in a loan contract, and the *Hikmat* of this law is to prevent exploitation. Prohibition of Riba is an *Illat*-driven rule, and thus the presence of this *Illat* necessitates abiding by the law irrespective of the existence of *Hikmat*. One can consider the analogy of alcohol consumption. Although the loss of consciousness is dependent on an individual's imperviousness that can vary from one person to another, alcohol is banned in every quantity, independent of the presence of its *Hikmat*. Similar is the case of compliance to the prohibition of Riba. It is an *Illat*-driven rule which should be decoupled from the presence of its *Hikmat*. Furthermore, Shariah makes no differentiation between the low or high rate or with reference to the purpose of loan, i. e., production or consumption.

As far as rich business persons are concerned, this would be rational only if all those indebted made considerably more money than the interest they pay. But since some make a loss, some earn very high amounts, and others earn lower amounts, this widens the gap between rich and poor. The argument, therefore, loses its ground.

13.4 Concluding remarks

The objections against the acceptance of contemporary Islamic banking presented in this chapter can be broadly summarized into three main recurring themes. The most frequently cited reasons relate to the justice and social welfare roles of Islamic banks. In fact, the top two criticisms of the respondents were that they considered Islamic banks to be exploitative as they played no role in the fulfillment of their social welfare duties. The second theme relates to the lack of distinction between Islamic and conventional banking in terms of instrument structures, and the third one questions the very need for Islamic banking in the modern age.

The discussion summarized above indicates that the objectives of Islamic banking as visualized by its critics are in contrast with the perception of its supporters. The critics focus on the societal role of Islamic banks and criticize their current commercial outlook that makes the distinction between them and their conventional counterparts difficult. The advocates, on the other hand, emphasize the removal of Riba and the production of real growth in the economy through asset-backed transactions.

Notes

1 Fairness in outcome without regard to the procedure involved in arriving at the outcome.
2 International Islamic fiqh academy is an academy for the advanced study of Islam which was established at the decision of the second summit of the Organisation of Islamic Cooperation. The council consists of Muslim world scholars and jurists who propose Islamic answers to the problems presented by the contemporary world.
3 Takaful is a Shariah compliant form of conventional insurance that is free from Riba, Gharar, and Maisir. It is based on the Quranic principles of mutual assistance. It is structured like a charitable pool of funds where each participant makes a regular contribution to the pool. The conviction behind this is to provide mutual protection and to share responsibility and risk in case one of the participants suffers a loss. The pool of funds is invested only in halal businesses.
4 Karachi interbank offered rate.

Bibliography

Ahmed, H. (2007). *Waqf-Based Microfinance: Realizing the Social Role of Islamic Finance*. Washington, DC: World Bank.

Asutay, M. (2007). Conceptualisation of the second best solution in overcoming the social failure of Islamic finance: Examining the overpowering of homoislamicus by homoeconomicus. *IIUM Journal in Economics and Management, 15*(2), 167–195.

Ayub, M. (2007). *Understanding Islamic Finance*. Chichester, UK: John Wiley & Sons.

Brau, J.C. & Woller, G.M. (2004). Microfinance: A comprehensive review of the existing literature. *Journal of Entrepreneurial Finance, 9*(1), 1–27.

Donaldson, T., & Dunfee, T.W. (1994). Toward a unified conception of business ethics: Integrative social contracts theory. *Academy of Management Review, 19*(2), 252–284.

Donaldson, T., & Dunfee, T.W. (1995). Integrative social contracts theory. *Economics and Philosophy, 11*(1), 85–112.

Dunfee, T.W. (2006). A critical perspective of integrative social contracts theory: Recurring criticisms and next generation research topics. *Journal of Business Ethics, 68*(3), 303–328.

Dusuki, A.W. (2008). Understanding the objectives of Islamic banking: A survey of stakeholders' perspectives. *International Journal of Islamic and Middle Eastern Finance and Management, 1*(2), 132–148.

El-Ashker, A.A.F. (1987). *The Islamic Business Enterprise*. London: Croom Helm.

Haron, S., & Hisham, B. (2003). Wealth mobilization by Islamic banks: The Malaysian case. Paper Presented at International Seminar on Islamic Wealth Creation. Durham, UK: University of Durham.

Hassan, N.M.N., & Musa, M. (2003). An evaluation of the Islamic banking development in Malaysia. Paper Presented at International Islamic Banking Conference 2003, Prato.

Khan, F. (2010). How 'Islamic' is Islamic banking? *Journal of Economic Behavior & Organization, 76*(3), 805–820.

Kuran, T. (1989). On the notion of economic justice in contemporary Islamic thought. *International Journal of Middle East Studies, 21*(2), 171–191.

Siddiqui, S.H. (2001). Islamic banking: True modes of financing. *New Horizon*. Retrieved from www.islamic-banking.com/iarticle_2.aspx.

Standard & Poor's (S&P). (2012). *Islamic Finance Outlook*. New York: Standard & Poor's Rating Service.

State Bank of Pakistan (SBP). (2014). *Strategic Plan: Islamic Banking Industry of Pakistan 2014–2018*.

Yurizk Research. (2013). *Global Islamic Finance Education Report*. Bear, DE: Yurizk Research.

Zaman, S.H. (1984). Definition of Islamic economics. *Journal of Research in Islamic Economics*, *1*(2), 49–50.

Chapter 14

Rethinking Islamic finance

An ethical perspective

A poor man walked in the room and asked his rich master for some money, a meager amount as a loan. He expressed his need and explained it in detail as if proving his sincerity. In that moment, I saw the rich master transform from an intellectual into a gladiator. Someone who had been wronged and was ready to fight to claim what was his. He reminded his servant of the debt that he owed to him, which was supposed to be paid off the month before. I was witnessing anger, outrage, and humiliation. It was a sharp contrast to the good natured man that I had known. He was screaming and threatening. The servant was scared, embarrassed, and hurt, leaving the room in shame and misery. I was in a state of surprise and shock, trying to understand the cause of this extreme reaction and questioned my friend. He started justifying his behavior with a clear consciousness as if he was the victim rather than the culprit. He expressed sentiments of self-righteousness and entitlement. As if his show of disapproval was a necessary reaction to avenge the harm that the servant had caused by usurping his money, his private property. The strong was exercising his power over the weak to set right the rules of the game. It seemed that the debt contract had given the lender a sense of self-righteousness and entitlement which justified the exercise of power. The entitlement had changed a civil human being into a perpetrator capable of inflicting violence. It seemed that the debt contract had created a class system of a borrower and a lender, or probably a lender and a defaulter, where violation of one's humanity became an acceptable act. In a hadith of the Prophet, to the nearest effect, it is said that the worst form of Riba is to disrespect a Muslim. Someone wise once said that the laws are made not for the criminals, who would always find a way to evade them; rather they are designed so good people do not become criminals. It may prevent the ordinary and the sincere, who might be tempted in their weaker moments to go against their good nature and succumb to the passion of their desires. That day I also realized that the privileged might find the debt contract as good and efficient, capable of increasing the welfare of the few. It may not affect them the way it may affect the poor and the needy. The laws of God are not made just for the rich and the successful but for all, not discriminating individuals based on their wealth. They are not made simply for the wise and the rational, the intelligent and the educated, but for all. The laws are made taking into account the best and worst of human nature, the nature that compels one to risk their lives to claim a petty benefit. The nature causes one to be obsessed with the immediate at the expense of the latter. The same nature that causes a sense of entitlement among the good people making them pursue acts of violence. The laws are designed not to serve human desires but to prevent the manifestations of their worst forms. Debt contract is apparently the realm of economics and finance, but these sciences do not deal with the good and the bad but only the fulfillment of desires in an efficient way. Hence, it is important that these simple means of exchange between individuals should also be governed by rules of ethics and religion rather than those of markets and efficiency.

14.1 Introduction

The dialogue between critics and supporters of Islamic banking narrated in the previous chapter tends to be fairly typical of that found in the literature where the debate has been raging for many years between Islamic scholars from both schools of thought. Both sides are quite uncompromising regarding their stances. This deadlock situation is actually harmful for the industry since it hinders the development of Islamic banking or of any improvement in the current practices. The entire scheme of Islamic economics within which Islamic banking sits is effectively intended to give a set of norms and principles which should be used as a guiding tool for all economic decision making. Individuals and institutions will be driven to take decisions which are not only in their own best interest but which will ensure that the interests of all of the impacted stakeholders and the society at large are also taken care of. In other words, Shariah provides the norms for ethical decision making. Ethics forms the core of every aspect of an Islamic society, and Muslims are required to be ethical in all of their activities. The ethical system of Islam, derived from the rule of Shariah, requires human beings to be just and socially responsible. In the context of business, the motives of a Muslim should not only be to make profit but also to be socially responsible. Anything that is good and beneficial to the society is halal and anything that causes menace is haram. 'Giving people their due right is the cardinal principle of Islamic ethics' (Ayub, 2007, 64). The Holy Quran and Sunnah provide guidelines that govern the rights and obligations of parties in a business transaction. 'Principles enunciating justice, mutual help, free consent and honesty on the part of the parties to a contract, avoiding fraud, misrepresentation and misstatement of facts and negation of injustice or exploitation provide grounds for valid contracts' (ibid.). Thus, Islamic economics is grounded in the rules of ethics. The question then arises: How can individuals who understand and even agree with the philosophy of Islamic economics actually stand at two extremes in

Table 14.1 Islamic banks vs conventional banks

Islamic banks	*Conventional banks*
Functions and operations are guided by sources of Shariah (Islamic Divine Law) namely the Quran and the Sunnah (traditions of the Prophet Muhammad p.b.u.h.)	Functions and operations are guided by secular principles and not based on any religious doctrines and values
Institutions that aim at balancing the profit-maximization doctrine and social responsibility	Institutions that emphasize on profit maximization
Financing instruments are based on either asset-backed trading contracts or equity financing with risk sharing	Financing instruments are based on interest-bearing mechanisms
Deposits are not interest oriented but profit-loss sharing oriented whereby investors' principal repayment is not guaranteed but entitled to a predetermined share of actual profit realized by the business	Deposits are interest oriented and the investor is assured of a pre-determined rate of interest with a guaranteed principal repayment
Islamic banks need to make charitable donations by paying zakat (compulsory religious levy) out of their income	There are no such requirements to undertake charitable activities
Islamic banks are prohibited from participating in economic activities which are unethical and prohibited by Shariah, such as businesses involving alcohol, prostitution, pork, environmental pollution, etc.	There are no such restrictions for conventional banks

Source: Dusuki (2008, 136, table I).

terms of their views on Islamic banking and at the same time consider their actions ethical in Islamic terms? Table 14.1 summarizes some of the key differences between Islamic and conventional banking. Table 14.2 highlights the main features of various Islamic financing tools.

14.2 Rethinking Islamic finance: an ethical framework

In order to find an answer to this question, this chapter explores a modern day ethical theory known as integrative social contract theory (ISCT). ISCT provides a unique framework for ethical decision making by considering the specific norms and practices of the communities impacted by the decision. It talks about two types of contracts against which ethical decisions need to be considered. The first is a theoretical *macrosocial* contract which brings together

Table 14.2 Features of various Islamic financing tools

Type of contract	*Guarantee*	*Rate of return*
Sale		
Murabaha	Collateral	Known
Musawamah	Collateral	Known
Leasing mode		
Ijarah	Collateral	Known
Sharing		
Musharakah	Penalty for misconduct	Unknown
Mudarabah	Penalty for misconduct	Unknown

Source: Ayub (2007, 77, table 4.1).

large communities of decision makers within universally accepted norms. The other is a real *microsocial* contract which binds individuals into smaller communities, for example, based on industry, culture, etc. The norms of the microcommunity, known as *authentic norms*, are tested against those of the larger macrocommunity, known as hypernorms, resulting in the emergence of community specific morally binding norms, known as *legitimate norms*. The theory states that all decision-making scenarios are then evaluated against these legitimate norms to ensure that they are ethical.

Based upon the results of the interviews, ISCT can be applied in the present context since the religion of Islam forms a macrocommunity bound together by the sole normative guidance source for Muslims, the Quran. While the entire Muslim community agrees on its significance, there is a difference of opinion regarding the interpretation of this text. This flexibility in interpretation has led to the formation of *microcommunities* within the *macrocontract* of Islam. These communities have their own set of authentic norms which become morally binding if they comply with all the relevant hypernorms of Islam. Hypernorms are those norms regarding which there is no ambiguity or room for interpretation and are acceptable as such by the entire Muslim community.

The arguments raised by the critics of Islamic banking and their rebuttals by the supporters suggest that both groups have formed into distinct microcommunities. They have thus developed their own authentic norms regarding the objectives of Islamic banking. A review of the literature on Islamic economics suggests that this understanding has been drawn with an incomplete focus on the norms of the wider Islamic society (called hypernorms) and, as a result, lacks moral legitimacy. Prohibitions of Riba, Gharar, and Maisir, along with social justice and welfare, are all hypernorms of an Islamic economic system. Those approving of Islamic banking are the ones who consider prohibition of Riba as the only hypernorm, and those critical of the practice focus solely on the norms of social responsibility and welfare.

This situation calls for rethinking Islamic finance on both sides—the supporters and the critics. They need to broaden their scope and focus on all the hypernorms of an Islamic economic system and understand that procedural and distributive justices together are integral to a just society. Islamic banks need to go beyond the literal meaning and legal interpretation of text and focus on social objectives as well. The current practice of Islamic banking involves solely the removal of Riba and ignores the systematic economic development and social justice action (Asutay, 2007). Thus, Islamic banks, in addition to the removal of Riba, need to incorporate in their philosophy a sensitivity toward the principles of economic justice and a willingness to apply those principles in the work that they undertake. Similarly, the critics should acknowledge that although it lacks some fundamentals of the Islamic economic system, Islamic banking today is indeed Riba free, which is a feature that effectively defines the Islamic economic system.

14.3 Integrative social contract theory

ISCT was introduced by Donaldson and Dunfee (1994). This theory is in contrast to other popular theories of ethics. For instance, the deontologist[1] and consequentialist[2] approaches and the popular stakeholder theory[3] operate at a high level of generality and fail to give guidance when it comes to solving specific moral quandaries across different cultures or traditions. The benefit of ISCT is that, rather than applying a universal set of ethical norms to decision-making scenarios, it appreciates the norms relevant to the particular decision maker. In other words, cultural norms, religious norms, industry norms, etc., are taken into consideration when determining how to make ethical business decisions. Therefore, what is ethical in one country or culture may be considered unethical in another. Similarly, ethical decision making in the context of a capitalist structure may not be considered ethical in an Islamic regime. ISCT attempts to integrate the normative[4] with the descriptive[5] by incorporating empirical findings within the contractarian process of making normative decisions. Until this theory, attempts at such an integration were not very fruitful (Donaldson & Dunfee, 1994). While the components of this theory have faced criticism over the years (see a review of critiques on ISCT by Dunfee, 2006), this theory is still the latest addition to the theories of business ethics and most relevant to the problem at hand.

ISCT is centered on two important concepts of *bounded moral rationality* and *social contracts*. At the outset, Donaldson and Dunfee make an important assumption stating that there are limits to the ability of decision makers when they apply moral theory to resolve ethical situations rationally. In other words, their *moral rationality* is somewhat constrained or *bounded*. The official term used by them is they have *bounded moral rationality*. They identify three reasons for this. Firstly, human beings lack the ability to capture and understand all issues related to a particular ethical dilemma. Secondly, ethical theories to date have failed to capture all moral issues in a single all-encompassing theory. Finally, the artifactual nature of economic systems implies that norms governing socioeconomic interactions vary from system to system and change with time, thus suggesting that ethical behavior is justified through system-specific or culture-specific appeals. The second key concept used in ISCT is that of social contracts. ISCT states that human beings enter into a theoretical contract with each other to devise normative rules of conduct. This contract is based upon the answer to the following question: *What certain rules would all rational contractors agree be applied to them in the context of economic transactions given they are not told what position they would occupy in that transaction* (Donaldson & Dunfee, 1995, 98)?[6]

These sets of rules, agreed between the contractors, make up what is known as the macrosocial contract. They are universal in nature and apply across all communities, cultures, and religions. ISCT makes a few assumptions while trying to come up with the rules that participants in the macrosocial contract will agree to. It first assumes that participants are aware of their own bounded rationality, and second, contracting parties share two desires: They want to satisfy their economic interest and also want to participate in communities that reflect their cultural and personal values. Considering these two assumptions, ISCT states that contractors will allow the right to devise more specific norms for themselves than can be devised by general morality. To explain this, let's go back to the point where ISCT says that rationality is bounded owing to the artifactual nature of systems. Given the desire of individuals to satisfy economic interests and given that this desire is best achieved through cooperative and group activity, individuals join organizations. The organizations that can best satisfy economic interests are the ones that have established standards of ethical conduct. This is because such norms need to be established if the organizations are to operate successfully so that there is no disagreement among members of what constitutes ethical conduct. Also in the pursuit of their economic interest, contractors want to keep their options open so that they can join the communities that best reflect their values, be they cultural or religious. For instance, a practicing Muslim might prefer to be involved in organizations where the norms are consistent with his faith. Thus, given this scenario and set of assumptions, macrocontractors will allow the existence of community-specific contracts that would regulate economic activity and lessen the negative effects of bounded moral rationality. These contracts are called microsocial contracts. They are less pervasive and specify norms of particular communities. Microsocial contracts exist between firms, informal groups and industries, etc. This freedom to devise norms for community-specific interactions is called the *moral free space*. Further, macrocontractors will allow the parties in the macrocontract the right to exit the communities and also makes their informed consent pertinent to the existence of microsocial contracts. Community-specific norms buttressed in consent of the members of the community are called authentic norms. However, these authentic norms don't have a moral authority. Macrocontractors realize that a community might agree on something that's against the very fundamental principles of human existence—for instance, a community might make killing human beings an authentic norm. Thus, to curb the possibility of relativism, macrocontractors want that norms decided at community level be tested against hypernorms to become morally binding. Hypernorms are the very fundamental principles of human *existence* that are used to evaluate community-level norms. They are the moral precepts for all and are relevant to all human beings irrespective of their cultural and religious differences. Once it is found that an authentic norm is not in violation with any hypernorm, that norm becomes legitimate for members of that community. It is very possible that as a result of this, different communities might have completely conflicting norms. Thus, to resolve the problem that would occur in a cross-community interaction, the terms of the macrosocial contract provide a set of principles called priority rules (for detailed explanation, see Donaldson & Dunfee, 1994) to decide which norm takes precedence. Priority is given to those norms that are more pervasive, consistent, and coherent within the framework of the macrosocial contract.

In summary, ISCT integrates two kinds of contracts. The first is a hypothetical contract called the macrosocial contract. It is a universal and more pervasive contract that allows communities significant moral free space to devise their own set of morally binding norms through formation of the second kind of contracts which are extant and are called microsocial contracts. However, the moral free space is constrained in three different ways by the terms of the macrosocial contract:

- through the requirement of consent at the community level;
- through the application of hypernorms;
- through the usage of priority rules to determine which norms gain precedence in case of conflicting legitimate norms.

14.4 Rethinking Islamic finance through ISCT

How can this be applied to the present situation where irreconcilably divergent views are held by members of the wider Islamic community who have formed smaller sub-communities of supporters and opposers of Islamic banking? In the previous chapter, critics of Islamic finance who were interviewed identified many issues that act as barriers to the widespread acceptance of Islamic banking and finance. Of all of the reasons given, the most frequently cited ones related to the social aspects of Islamic banking and the inability (or failure) of Islamic financial institutions to address these, while the original theory states that the macrosocial contract is upon a level that transcends religious and cultural boundaries and allows for the existence of microcontracts based on religious and cultural preferences.

It is common knowledge that Islam is not a monolithic religion. A religion of 1.6 billion people spread out across the globe, it is inevitable that they have differences of opinion and interpretation of textual sources. This results in diversity of economic rules that vary wherever Muslims reside—as a result, its members cannot be confined to a single microcommunity within the larger macrocontract of humanity. Having said that, it needs to be considered that its members do share some norms and believes; for instance, Tauheed (the oneness of Allah) is a concept that is unanimously accepted among Muslims. Thus, there is a hypothetical macrosocial contract that binds Muslims all over the world through norms that are accepted without any opposition. How are microcommunities created within this contract? While the sole normative guidance source for Muslims is the Quran and every person places his or her faith in the text, the interpretation of this text varies among Muslims—for instance, while there is no difference of opinion regarding praying, the way prayer is conducted can be different. There is a body of Muslims who believe that while standing in *Aqamah*, hands should be on the chest, whereas some believe they should be on the sides. This leeway of interpretation is the moral free space in our context. Thus, within the macrosocial contract, Muslims make microcommunities to lessen the effects of bounded moral rationality. Bounded moral rationality is defined, in this scenario, as the inability of Muslims to capture all information related to a problem and to directly apply the guidance of the Quran to that problem. This formation of microcommunities explains the existence of sects among Muslims at a bigger level. Hence, Muslims, based on their interpretations of the holy text, make microcommunities with their own authentic norms. However, these norms would have moral authority/legitimacy if and only if they comply with all the relevant hypernorms specified for that particular problem. Hypernorms are the principles of economic conduct among Muslims that are absolutely clear with no room for interpretation. Hence, their existence is accepted as such by all the communities of Muslims.

The interplay of the arguments between the critics and supporters of contemporary Islamic banking on the issue of socioeconomic objectives of the practice suggests that each is a microcommunity within the macrosocial contract of Islamic economics. They have established their own understanding of ethical behavior for Islamic banks through placing emphasis on their own sets of authentic norms. But these individual authentic norms are not legitimate/morally binding as their compliance is with a few hypernorms of an Islamic economic system. Welfare of the community, social justice, and prohibitions of Riba, Gharar, and Maisir, as indicated earlier, are all hypernorms of the Islamic economic system, but the two groups under scrutiny put an incomplete focus on these norms.

The authentic norm of critics of Islamic finance is distributive justice, which is why they only focus on the hypernorms of social justice and welfare of community and argue that the purpose of Islamic banking is to ensure economic and social welfare of the community. They say that Islamic banks should play their role in the creation of a just and exploitation free society by regulating the distribution of income and taking care of the financially disadvantaged. The authentic norm of adherents, on the other hand, is procedural justice and thus they place their emphasis on the hypernorm of prohibitions and consider prohibition of Riba and the production of real growth in the economy as the objective of Islamic banking. They place stress on the benefits of asset-backed transactions and risk-based capital. This contrast in focus has led to a dubious understanding of the 'Islamic' nature of contemporary Islamic banking (see Figure 14.1).

Since both critics and supporters are testing their authentic norms only against a few of the hypernorms and not all, their norms are only authentic

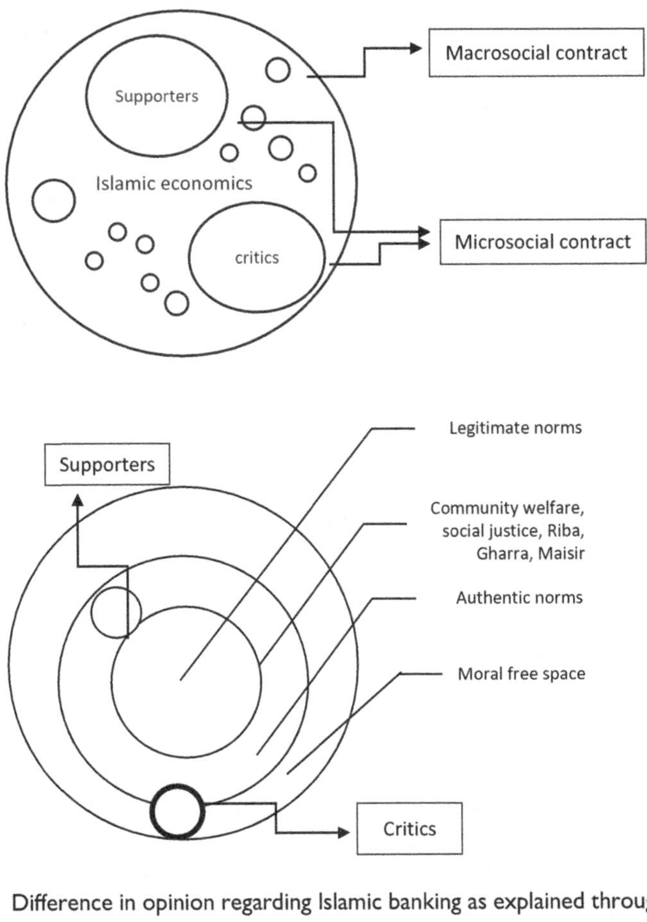

Figure 14.1 Difference in opinion regarding Islamic banking as explained through ISCT

and lack moral authority. Their norms would become legitimate only when they comply with all the hypernorms of the Islamic economic system. The next section suggests a way to deal with this deadlock situation.

14.5 Way forward

In order to bridge the gap between the interpretations of the critics and supporters regarding Islamic banking's socioeconomic objectives, a fundamental rethinking is required on both sides. Instead of a partial focus on some hypernorms, both need to broaden their scope and consider all of the hypernorms of Islamic economics.

14.5.1 Supporters

Although *Adl* and *Ihsan* are at the foundation of an Islamic financial system (Khan, 2010; Siddiqi, 2004), and socioeconomic justice, equitable distribution of income, and eradication of poverty are the goals of Islam (Ahmed, 2007), current Islamic banking is not entirely representative of these ideas. Islamic finance today, instead of being rooted in the principles of Islamic political economy, is just about the removal of Riba (Asutay, 2007). 'Rather than being part of the Islamic political economy, IBF has been pursuing policies away from the theoretical underpinnings and systemic understanding of Islamic economics and has located a surrogate financial framework in neoclassical economics' (Asutay, 2007, 169).

While the Islamic finance industry has grown at an amazing pace and the operations and modes of Islamic financing have increased, the lives of common Muslims have not been improved (Asutay, 2007). The reason for this is the dependence on making practices and instruments Shariah compliant rather than Shariah based. Islamic banks need to adopt a value-oriented approach and introduce social banking to correct their social failures (Asutay, 2007) so that the practices are consistent with all of the legitimate norms of an Islamic economic system. One possible way of doing this is to enhance the focus on Islamic microfinance (Ahmed, 2007; Yurizk, 2013). Conventional microfinance charges high rates of interest and has failed to eradicate poverty in many areas (Brau & Woller, 2004). An emphasis on microfinance will help Islamic banks in achieving their objective of distributive justice.

14.5.2 Critics

Valid arguments have been raised against the current system of Islamic banking. The Islamic banking industry appears to be as much focused on profit maximization as the conventional side, and Islamic banks today are not fulfilling the hypernorms of social welfare and social justice. However, a prerequisite for accomplishing full distributive justice is the fulfillment of the conditions of procedural justice. While there is still a long way to go, some significant milestones (such as the elimination of Riba) have been achieved, and as more procedural conditions are satisfied, Islamic banking will continue to move along the spectrum and become more equitable as intended under Shariah.

14.6 Concluding remarks

Islamic banking and finance is growing at a tremendous rate throughout the world. However, any further progress of this industry is dependent on both sides (supporters and critics) coming together and entering into a dialogue to understand different perspectives. The understanding and appreciation of the gaps of the discipline will pave the way for improvement. Using ISCT, we have noted that microcommunities have developed within the large Islamic economic community and are placing an emphasis on a different set of authentic norms for ethical decision making. This has resulted in two starkly different views as to how 'Islamic' is contemporary Islamic banking. Whereas the advocates of contemporary Islamic banking focus on the norm of prohibition of Riba—equating this elimination to procedural justice—the critics focus on the norms of social responsibility and equitable distribution of wealth, i.e., distributive justice.

Going forward, the concerns regarding Islamic banking can be removed if critics and proponents of contemporary Islamic banking, instead of concentrating on some of the norms, focus on all of the hypernorms of an Islamic economic society. The critics need to become more considerate of the role of Islamic banks and appreciate the fact that contemporary Islamic banking is ensuring procedural justice in society. The Islamic banks on the other hand need to realize their social responsibility so they can replicate the ideology of a true Islamic economic system.

Notes

1 According to this approach, an act is morally correct if the act itself complies with certain rules. One could cite Kantian deontology in the same vein.
2 In this approach, the rightness or wrongness of an act is dependent only on the end result of that act. Popular examples of this approach are egoism and utilitarianism.
3 Interests of all stakeholders need to be taken into account when making a decision.
4 How things should be.
5 How things are in reality.
6 To understand this, imagine you are part of a buy-sell arrangement. What kind of principal rules or codes of conduct would you want such a transaction to have if you are not told whether you will be a buyer or a seller.

Bibliography

Ahmed, H. (2007). *Waqf-Based Microfinance: Realizing the Social Role of Islamic Finance.* World Bank.

Asutay, M. (2007). Conceptualisation of the second best solution in overcoming the social failure of Islamic finance: Examining the overpowering of homoislamicus by homoeconomicus. *IIUM Journal in Economics and Management, 15* (2), 167–195.

Ayub, M. (2007). *Understanding Islamic Finance*. Chichester, UK: John Wiley & Sons.

Brau, J.C., & Woller, G.M. (2004). Microfinance: A comprehensive review of the existing literature. *Journal of Entrepreneurial Finance, 9* (1), 1–27.

Donaldson, T., & Dunfee, T.W. (1994). Toward a unified conception of business ethics: Integrative social contracts theory. *Academy of Management Review, 19* (2), 252–284.

Donaldson, T., & Dunfee, T.W. (1995). Integrative social contracts theory. *Economics and Philosophy, 11* (1), 85–112.

Dunfee, T.W. (2006). A critical perspective of integrative social contracts theory: Recurring criticisms and next generation research topics. *Journal of Business Ethics, 68* (3), 303–328.

Dusuki, A.W. (2008). Understanding the objectives of Islamic banking: A survey of stakeholders' perspectives. *International Journal of Islamic and Middle Eastern Finance and Management, 1* (2), 132–148.

El-Ashker, A.A.F. (1987). *The Islamic Business Enterprise*. London: Croom Helm.

Haron, S., & Hisham, B. (2003). Wealth mobilization by Islamic banks: The Malaysian case. Paper Presented at International Seminar on Islamic Wealth Creation, Durham, UK: University of Durham.

Hassan, N.M.N., & Musa, M. (2003). An evaluation of the Islamic banking development in Malaysia. Paper Presented at International Islamic Banking Conference 2003, Prato, Italy.

Khan, F. (2010). How 'Islamic' is Islamic banking? *Journal of Economic Behavior & Organization, 76* (3), 805–820.

Kuran, T. (1989). On the notion of economic justice in contemporary Islamic thought. *International Journal of Middle East Studies, 21* (2), 171–191.

Siddiqui, S.H. (2001). Islamic banking: True modes of financing. *New Horizon*. Retrieved from www.islamic-banking.com/iarticle_2.aspx.

Standard & Poor's (S&P). (2012). *Islamic Finance Outlook*. Standard & Poor's Rating Service.

State Bank of Pakistan (SBP). (2014). *Strategic Plan: Islamic Banking Industry of Pakistan*. 2014–2018.

Yurizk Research. (2013). *Global Islamic Finance Education Report*. Bear, DE: Yurizk Research.

Zaman, S.H. (1984). Definition of Islamic economics. *Journal of Research in Islamic Economics, 1* (2), 49–50.

Chapter 15

Conclusion

"The stage was set, the dignitaries had arrived. The grandeur was visible, the audience was elated. The seats were filled with the who's who of the Islamic finance industry. It was an event that not many wanted to miss. The smartest academics, the pragmatic bankers, and the powerful regulators were all present to discuss the future of the Islamic finance industry. The pursuit of the noble cause, along with the opportunity to network and rise in the career ladder, meant that the hall was full of the sincere and the ambitious. The event was to start with the keynote address of one of the biggest names in the Islamic finance industry. The person whose identity is hidden for the purposes of anonymity, sat in his chair with a sense of certainty and inner security. He seemed to not experience the nerves that one would associate with such an event. The presence of the powerful did not unnerve him. His name was called by the organizer and he moved with his usual sense of self-assurance and grace, not in the least bit giving away the shock waves he was about to create. The greatest champion of Islamic finance was about to unleash carnage on it. A sincere destruction, meant to restore its authenticity rather than bringing permanent damage. His words were imbued with rhyme and reason, invigorating the souls of a few while bringing horror to the faces of the others. His words were those of a man driven by a cause which was not unadulterated by the pursuit of money. Notions of profit, risk, and efficiency seemed alien to him; the bigger purpose seemed to be the singular drive. The crowd could hear the roar of a man who believed in the absolute prohibition of Riba. He believed from the depth of his being that Islamic finance was an 'alternative' designed to dominate the prohibited, not to succumb to its whims and never to co-exist. His words were not those of a critic bent to questioning the legitimacy of the industry; they were the war cry of a warrior who believed in the immense potential of a thing only to watch it painfully settle for a meager victory. He believed in establishing an alternative way of dealing imbued with the ideal of fairness and justice, with the intention of achieving God's pleasure, rather than simply following the outer form of religiosity. The intellectual in him knew that the outer form was better than no form, but his mystical side yearned for the spirit. Many a time in the past he had thought that the soul could not exist without the body, the outer form of Islamic finance serving as the body. The outer precedes the inner. This day he longed for the inner reality at the expense of annihilating the form that he had created with much labor and care. It seemed that the heart had refused to listen to the mind. The shackles of propriety were broken by the tearful emotion of being. The deepest desire, unmet for so long, controlled by the strength of resolve, was impossible to manage. It seemed like the words of a dying man, whose only wish in life was under the threat of un-fulfillment. The pain in his voice would remain undetected unless one could view life from his perspective, otherwise the emotion he was experiencing would remain elusive. His words were a plea as much to the people as to God. It was a sermon as well as a prayer. It touched many in the audience; for others it was no more a voice of impracticality, utopian ideas devoid of practical relevance. Some shrugged them off immediately as they would be incapable of generating money for them. For others it brought applause, a standing ovation that brought about fleeting emotions rather than permanent change.

After the address I met another scholar of the field, someone with a deep appreciation for our keynote speaker, yet a man of reason and rationality. In a hushed voice, bringing his mouth closer to my ear, as if making a confession, he reiterated what many in the industry had come to believe all along, that some visionaries fail to see their dreams and desires become reality. The realization that Islamic finance would take a reality different from what it presently professed would remain wishful thinking. These were the words of a pragmatic, who had seen the worst of human nature. He realized that fulfillment of the deep desires of the customers was as important as legal compliance. The growth of the Islamic finance industry had more to do with fulfillment of the desires for gain, in the guise of the promise of fulfilling religious law. He reminded me that Islamic finance was the triumph of the human passion, with the spark of religion. But religion only remained a spark and not the fire required for change.

That event left me with a perennial question: How should one respond to a state of existence which seemed a huge improvement to the alternative yet falls short of what was expected? It feels like an uneasy pleasure where joy and celebrations co-exist with despair and disappointment. The thought that the alternative is so much worse brings relief and contentment, while the feeling that the present could have been so much better is accompanied with anger and frustration. Apparently, the future direction provides the only hope. A future that promises the fulfillment of unmet expectations brings joy to the present. The inadequacies of the present are easy to ignore with the realization that in a distant future, at a date unknown, lurking around the corner, what is left to be done would be done. The nonexistent would come to exist and what is absent would emerge. The proponents of Islamic finance for many years have claimed that the distant future is not so distant, when the patience would be rewarded and the industry would emerge into something much more than it".

This book is an outcome of our dissatisfaction with the Islamic finance literature. This realization confronted us as clearly as day during an academic conference which saw the presentation of many papers on Islamic finance. The brightest researchers who had labored for many years were showcasing their work, anchoring their ideas in the existing literature, and employing rigorous methodologies—the fancy tests, the unique data sets, and the ephemeral claim that 'this has never been done before'. Each paper claimed to contribute significantly to the body of knowledge, creating an astounding feeling that there should not be any gaps left in our understanding of Islamic finance.

Quite a few papers were critical of the role of bankers, regulators, and Shariah advisors as if they had deceived the entire world. They were held responsible for making people believe against their wills that something which was utterly unacceptable is grounded in the revealed text. The difference between Islamic and un-Islamic or conventional was marginalized, creating reasonable doubt as to whether Islamic finance is really Islamic or, worse, whether conventional finance is really un-Islamic. Many of these academics, who were good at giving words to individual feelings, were expressing the common psyche of the society which was full of doubts regarding the Islamic finance industry. It felt as if the custodians of values were applying the test of reason and passing judgement on the field. Ironically, apart from the critics who held the field responsible for the ills of the Muslim world, the conference saw exuberant young researchers who were trying to test outdated and largely irrelevant econometric models using Islamic finance data. The apparent purpose was to identify the value Islamic finance creates beyond assuaging religious dissatisfaction and the curiosity of its customers. In the guise of defending the cause of Islamic finance, the ambition to publish and get tenured was obvious for the keen eye.

Quite a few papers were devoted to finding strategies that investors or customers could apply to increase their profitability. This could have been an important contribution; unfortunately, most of the strategies proposed or methods employed were so distant from the world of reality that making use of them should remain more of a theoretical construct. The work of fellow academics left us with a sense of unease and a need for reflection. Islamic finance academics have been critical of practitioners; but is it not about time that we subjected ourselves to that same sharp perception? We need to ask ourselves how our research and findings help in explaining the reality of Islamic finance and whether the understanding in any way can help reshape it.

Islamic finance has given us much to celebrate. To the believers it offers a sense of comfort that their choices are no more self-sacrificing. They can be true to their desires and their God. The connection of the Islamic financial product, no matter how weak, to the revealed text makes it virtuous. The label 'Shariah compliant' reduces the inner conflict that we experience against our own selves. It helps to resolve the battle within. Our relationship with humanity and the universe at large—for now, Islamic finance alludes these conflicts. However, in due course these would have to be addressed. For academics, Islamic finance offers a cause much greater than scholarly reputation—the curiosity it offers to attempt to understand Divine wisdom and intent.

Index